The Mechanical Feature

The Mechanical Feature

*100 Years of Engineering
at Mississippi State University*

C. JAMES HAUG

PUBLISHED FOR THE
MISSISSIPPI STATE UNIVERSITY COLLEGE OF ENGINEERING
BY THE
UNIVERSITY PRESS OF MISSISSIPPI

All photographs in this book have been reproduced from Mississippi State University Publications.

Copyright © 1992 by Mississippi State University
All rights reserved
Manufactured in the United States of America

The paper in this book meets the guidelines for permanence and durability of the Committee on Production Guidelines for Book Longevity of the Council on Library Resources.

Library of Congress Cataloging-in-Publication Data

Haug, C. James, 1946-
   The mechanical feature : 100 years of engineering at Mississippi State University / C. James Haug.
     p. cm.
   Includes bibliographical references (p.   ) and index.
   ISBN 0-87805-561-4 (alk. paper)
   1. Mississippi State University. College of Engineering.
I. Title.
T171.M7H38   1992
620'.0071'1762953—dc20   91-48006
                                                                    CIP

British Library Cataloging-in-Publication data available

For the

Mississippi State University faculty members

who persevered

Contents

Preface ix

CHAPTER ONE   Establishing the Mechanical Feature   3
CHAPTERTWO   The Challenges of Growth   22
CHAPTER THREE The Struggle for Survival   43
CHAPTER FOUR   Toward National Recognition   62
CHAPTER FIVE   The Birth of a Modern College   79
CHAPTER SIX   The Research University   100

Notes 127
Bibliography 148
Index 156

Preface

Although the College of Engineering at Mississippi State has traditionally been one of the university's major units, its history has never been documented. The primary purpose of this book, therefore, is to examine the history of the college as it approaches its one hundredth anniversary in 1992. A more general purpose of the book is to provide insight into the nature of higher education in Mississippi viewed from an operational perspective. This book, therefore, is a study in institutional and administrative history, a genre which is becoming ever more significant in our age of bureaucracy. Post-secondary education in Mississippi has been explored before from several points of view, but these studies have almost always concentrated on the work of political or educational leaders. This book examines higher education in Mississippi from the perspective of the actors, not the directors.

There are many pitfalls to be avoided in writing a book such as this. Historians engaged in institutional studies often find themselves on a slippery slope marked with many opportunities to escape critical reflection. It is sometimes hard to avoid the comfortable rest stations tended by the chroniclers, the antiquarians, and the celebrators. They will always provide a pleasant welcome, and it is tempting to enter their doors. Such visits must be avoided, however, because for institutional history to be valuable to a wider audience, it is necessary to take a critical approach and place it in a broader perspective. Thus, this book is an effort to place the history of engineering at Mississippi State in the context of the history of administration, the history of technology, and the history of American higher education.

The history of education in the South has been generally neglected in comparison to other regions of the United States, and technological education in particular has received relatively little attention. There are a variety of reasons for this neglect that range from the South's poverty to its agrarian tradition; from its heritage of segregation, to the legacy of social and intellectual isolation in the aftermath of the Civil War. Taken together these themes explain much of the South's uniqueness. They have contributed to the formation of the South's splendid literary heritage as well as to its suspicion of modernization. They certainly have had a major impact on the region's institutions of higher education.

These forces have been especially pronounced in Mississippi, a state which has usually been found at the bottom of most lists reflecting material wealth. Mississippi's leaders have seldom possessed much appreciation or understanding of the nature of higher education at the national level, and have traditionally tended to look inward for inspiration, viewing outside modernizing forces such as urbanization and industrialization with suspicion. Consequently, higher education, which by its very nature encourages students to learn to understand unfamiliar issues and ideas, to become less insular, and to assume a broad, urbane perspective, has never been a main priority in Mississippi, and the state's institutions have always suffered from neglect and chronic underfunding. Thus, engineering education at Mississippi State has had much to overcome in order to provide superior technical education. In order to maintain academic respectability Mississippi's institutions and their faculty members have had to be very creative and persistent in coping with a level of adversity that was often extreme.

Against the background of the College of Engineering's constant struggle with adversity, this study focuses on several different themes. First, throughout much of its history the college was engaged in a struggle for survival. Established in a rural state with little sympathy to industry, which was never willing to adequately support higher education, engineering educators at Mississippi State generally found themselves teaching students with insufficient facilities, equipment, or salaries. Overcoming these vicissitudes, most of which were probably shared by others engaged in higher education in Mississippi, was a formidable task requiring extraordinary levels of creativity. The book also examines the problems faced by the College of Engineering in developing a nationally recognized curriculum and research program. Faced with the dilemma of attempting to conform to national accreditation standards, and at the same time accommodating the demands of Mississippians for an extremely practical education at a very low cost, the college regularly engaged in intense debate over the kind of education it was expected to provide. The development of this theme provides insight into the arguments over curriculum and instruction that have divided engineering educators at all levels throughout the twentieth century. Finally, this study considers the intricacies involved in the administration of higher education in Mississippi viewed from a grass-roots perspective that provides insight into the general operation and development of higher education in the South.

This book emerged from conversations with Dr. Robert Altenkirch, Dean of the College of Engineering at Mississippi State University, who encouraged me to consider writing a critical history of the College of Engineering at Mississippi State. Throughout the life of the project he has been very helpful and supportive.

Many people have provided assistance in obtaining documents and research materials. The staff of Mississippi State's Mitchell Memorial Library was always helpful. I especially acknowledge the assistance of archivist Michael Ballard and assistant archivist Betty Self, who always went the extra step in locating documents. Lynn Mueller and Mattie Sink of the Department of Special Collections helped to locate materials on the history of Mississippi. Jane Flowers and Linda Tuck of the College of Engineering staff ironed out administrative details and found documents that had not yet made their way to the university archives. Peggy Bonner, Lona Reinecke, and Karen Groce of the department of history provided outstanding document preparation assistance.

I am also deeply indebted to the student assistants who have assisted me during the book's various stages. While completing my research and writing, I often thought of Professors Albert Barnes and Charles Edgar Ard who, at the turn of the century, headed the departments of mechanical and electrical engineering, carried heavy teaching loads, and at the same time operated the entire campus system of services with only the assistance of undergraduate students. Mississippi State undergraduates who have helped in the data-entry and document preparation aspects of the project are Showanda Harbin and Veronica Gamble. Graduate students who provided research assistance are Charlotte Owens, Michael McCarty, Alison White, and especially, Loralee Davenport.

A number of past and present Mississippi State University administrators and faculty members have provided information about the College of Engineering and the university. Robert Altenkirch, Willie McDaniel, Harry

Simrall, Dean Colvard, and others mentioned in the bibliography all gave generously of their time, and have provided valuable insight into the recent history of the College of Engineering. All historical interpretations and judgements are, however, my own. Errors, of course, are also my responsibility.

My final thanks must go to my wife Ruth and my sons Stopher, Marty, and Jimmy who were always supportive, and cheerfully tolerated the by-products of research and writing such as unusually large piles of paper and books, missed vacations, and the company of a sometimes cantankerous author.

The Mechanical Feature

CHAPTER ONE

Establishing the Mechanical Feature

Engineering education at Mississippi State University and at the seventy-one land-grant institutions throughout the United States and its territories began in 1862 largely as the result of legislation known as the Morrill Act. The name Justin Smith Morrill has become synonymous with practical higher education in the United States. Morrill was a representative and later a senator from Vermont. Although most of his political career was devoted to using the power of the federal government to promote the interests of American industry by maintaining a hard currency and high tariffs, he gradually became obsessed with the idea of using public lands to promote higher education for "the industrial classes," and his enduring fame rests on this initiative.[1]

For the most part Morrill's economic and social ideas were anathema to Southern politicians who opposed subsidies for Northern industries and favored soft money and low prices for imports. Southerners opposed Morrill's educational schemes as well because they seemed to involve an excessive amount of federal interference in state affairs, and because Southerners generally saw higher education as the prerogative of the wealthy. They also knew that the main constituencies for Morrill's programs, including his land-grant college idea, were the industrial and agricultural interests of the Northeast. Thus, Southern politicians had fought Morrill's proposals for years until 1857, when a land-grant act passed, only to be vetoed by President James Buchanan as impractical and unconstitutional.[2]

The Civil War removed Southern opponents of land-grant legislation from the Congress, and in 1862 President Abraham Lincoln signed Morrill's cherished legislation into law. According to the provisions of the Morrill Act, each state received 30,000 acres of land for each senator and representative from the state to support colleges where the study of agriculture and the mechanic arts would be emphasized and which would specifically "promote the liberal and practical education of the industrial classes in the several pursuits and professions in life." The act did not initially apply to states in rebellion, and Mississippi did not receive its share until 1871. It divided the money received from the sale of 210,000 acres of land between the University of Mississippi and the newly-founded Alcorn University which was to provide higher education for the state's blacks. The Reconstruction government allotted three-fifths of the land-grant monies to Alcorn and two-fifths to the University of Mississippi.[3]

Before passage of the Morrill Act the curriculum of the University of Mississippi, like that of most institutions of higher education in the United States, was devoted almost entirely to the study of the liberal arts. Students took courses in the classics, philosophy, religion, mathematics, and science. In essence, the faculty assumed that its purpose was to produce a graduate who could enter the ministry or another profession that did not require one to work with his hands. Although the University of Mississippi made minor revisions in its curriculum in 1871 in order to make itself eligible for land-grant funds, its programs remained almost entirely based on the liberal arts.[4]

Mississippi in the nineteenth century was a predominantly agricultural state, and the state's farmers had long been interested in persuading the University of Mississippi to provide some kind of technical education. During the 1850s the state legislature made special appropriations to what it optimistically called the Agricultural and Zoological Science Department at the university, although this department existed only in the imaginations of lawmakers. In 1856 the legislature urged the university to add an agricultural division to its existing five, a move which it passively resisted, using money appropriated for this purpose to add to its collection of scientific equipment.[5] Thus, Chancellor John N. Waddel's move to establish departments of agriculture and mechanics met with a great deal of skepticism from the university's faculty and students. Ample evidence that the university was better prepared to polish the rough edges from the sons of Mississippi's aristocracy than to offer education to the children of the industrial classes surfaced when courses in agricultural education were offered: No students appeared to take the courses. After a brief unsuccessful struggle to make the program work, the university abandoned it in 1876. The program in the mechanic arts fared little better. Although the university offered a degree in civil engineering, only a handful of students took the courses.[6]

It is not entirely clear why the effort to establish agricultural and mechanical education at the University of Mississippi failed. Although Chancellor Waddel was committed to the program and had hired Eugene Hilgard, a well-trained scientist, to supervise the program, most of the classically trained faculty were unsympathetic. At least that is what Stephen D. Lee, the first president of Mississippi A & M, thought. Lee chastised the established institutions for taking federal funds and using them to build up the existing departments. In Lee's eyes such behavior was treating agriculture and the mechanic arts as "poor kin at the rich folks' house.". It is also likely that the students at the University of Mississippi, most of whom were the sons of Mississippi planters, found the agricultural and mechanical arts program contemptible. John Crumpton Hardy, the third president of Mississippi A & M, found this explanation most satisfactory. In the South, he explained to a Canadian correspondent, it was essential to keep agricultural and mechanical programs separate from the traditional universities because of "the great prejudice against manual labor on account of the institution of slavery" and that it was "absolutely impossible to develop the two together."[7]

In addition people were beginning to demand an alternative to what they viewed as elitist higher education. This attitude was evident in an address delivered by F. T. Cooper to the Mississippi Teachers' Institute in 1879. Schools that provided practical training, he told his audience, were vastly more important than traditional colleges or universities, where "the pupil is generally facilitated in the development of his taste for cigars, wines, baseball tournaments, yachting matches, fine clothes, excursions, spending money, and gentlemanly leisure."

> I must not dwell upon the girl of the period, as she sits before her $500 piano, tied down with the remorseless pin-back, an abject slave of the most exacting tyrant. . . . What can you expect of her? How much has she cost and what is she fit for? Can she milk a cow? Can she make a biscuit?

Can she sew a button on a shirt? Does she sweep the house? Does she know how to wash dishes? In a word, does she know any practical thing whatever?[8]

Moved by the failure of agricultural and mechanical education in Oxford, the legislature of 1878 removed the land-grant funds from the University of Mississippi and established a new College of Agriculture and the Mechanic Arts for whites in addition to reorganizing Alcorn University in order to make it an A & M college for blacks.[9] The legislature established a board of trustees to oversee the new college, which was to be a "first-class institution at which the youth of the State of Mississippi may acquire a common school education and a scientific and practical knowledge of agriculture, horticulture and the mechanic arts . . . without excluding the scientific and classical studies, including military tactics."[10]

After much deliberation the college's nine-member board of trustees selected Starkville as a location from among a number of towns in east Mississippi. It remains unclear why Starkville won out in the highly political selection process, although Colonel W. B. Montgomery, a member of the first board of trustees seems to have been instrumental. Montgomery used his considerable political skills to cajole members of the board into supporting his hometown, and torpedoed the bid of Starkville's main rival, Meridian, by emphasizing that city's "dubious moral climate," which he thought would be deleterious to the character of the boys attending the new college. Anecdotal descriptions of Starkville from the period provide little insight into the selection process. One traveler called it a "sprightly little city," while another observer wrote that it had "the deepest mud and hardest water to be found anywhere." A board member who perhaps was unconsciously stating the real reason why the Trustees decided to locate the college in Starkville described it as "a quiet country town, its people and community exceptionally sober and conservative."[11]

The board chose Stephen D. Lee, a native of South Carolina who had distinguished himself during the Civil War, rising to the rank of lieutenant general, to lead the college. Although Lee had not been raised in an agricultural family, he went into farming after the Civil War and for ten years operated a plantation in Noxubee County owned by his wife. His farming experience was disastrous, and he left agriculture around 1876, a victim of high interest rates, low cotton prices, and an undependable supply of labor.[12]

Lee's depressing experience as a cotton planter undoubtedly influenced his policies as president of Mississippi A & M. His overall goal was to use the power of education to put agriculture on a more businesslike basis than had been done traditionally in the South. In what seems an incongruous statement for a Confederate general, Lee advocated breaking up large plantations, which he thought uneconomical, and selling the smaller farms to immigrants from the North who would somehow be persuaded to come to Mississippi with their capital and skills. "Speedier and better results will follow from the introduction of Northern immigrants into our midst," wrote Lee, "than from any other source."[13]

One of the first tasks facing Lee and the board of trustees was developing a curriculum for the new college. This was neither simple nor easy because, while the spirit of the Morrill Act was clear, the language defining its implementation was not. There was no doubt that the new colleges created by the act were supposed to benefit the "industrial classes" which traditionally had no access to existing institutions of higher education. The act decreed that these colleges provide learning related to agriculture and the mechanic arts, but it also asked them to promote "liberal and practical education" and to fit their students for "the several pursuits and professions in life." The Mississippi legislature had further admonished the new colleges not to ignore scientific and classical studies. Justin Morrill's thoughts provided some guidance—he had encouraged colleges to "lop off a portion [of the] old useless classics," but the land-grant colleges founded before 1878 generally had adopted a traditional curriculum, simply adding the "practical studies" to it, usually on an elective basis.[14] In practice, therefore, the board knew that its new land-grant college could offer whatever curriculum it wished as long as it offered some kind of practical education oriented toward the children of the industrial classes.

Lee did not allow himself to be confused by the ambiguities of the Morrill Act or of the legislative mandate and attempted to shape the curriculum in accordance with his own convictions. Aware that agriculture in Mississippi was "deplorable and growing worse every year," he became convinced that formal agricultural education was a large part of the solution to Mississippi's problems. Lee's first faculty included men who could teach "Scientific and Practical Agriculture and Horticulture," chemistry and physics, and "Horticulture, Botany, and Animal and Vegetable Physiology." It also included faculty members who could teach the classical side of the curriculum such as

G. S. Roudebush, head of the English Department, W. J. T. Sullivan, principal of the Preparatory School, and J. A. Bailey, head of the Department of Ancient Languages. They were later joined by a professor of mathematics and several faculty members who were employed in the preparatory department to provide remedial training for students not ready for college-level work.[15]

Lee emphasized his dedication to agriculture in his inaugural address on October 6, 1880. He told his audience how large the agricultural classes were in the state and nation and how disadvantaged farmers were compared to those in other occupations who had special colleges of their own to provide training. The A & M College, said Lee, was to be operated "primarily with a view to the teaching and fostering of agricultural and mechanical arts, together with all the cognate pursuits that flow out of them and that are allied to them. . . . The great sustaining industry of the State," he concluded, "is to be lifted to the high plane of liberal and humanizing pursuits."[16] It was wrong, he later wrote, to require the sons of farmers to be educated in the "hard school of experience" when "the favored boy who will be a doctor, engineer, lawyer or professional man is carefully educated." Indeed, "the professional farmer has more need of a good education than anyone else, for he has to inquire of nature her secrets and he must understand the natural sciences, and must have the liberal learning necessary to comprehend them." It also was important, Lee thought, to provide an education to children whose parents were not wealthy. "This is a great advance in education," he wrote, "when our beloved State puts it in the power of her boys to have a College education for less than $100 a year."[17]

Lee soon found, however, that the faculty and students of the new institution were at least as interested in traditional education as they were in learning about agriculture. Several members of the tiny new faculty were traditionalists who insisted that the college offer studies in the classical and liberal arts. Roudebush, Sullivan, and Bailey vigorously opposed Lee's agricultural emphasis and attempted to make the curriculum as liberal as possible. They probably were supported by the students. Most of the 354 students who appeared for the first session were from Starkville, Aberdeen, Columbus, or Macon. Many of them seemed interested mainly in preparing themselves for urban professions, not for farming. Lee's own son, Blewitt, was not untypical. After leaving Mississippi A & M as a member of the first graduating class, he went to Harvard to earn a law degree. Of the eighty-eight men who graduated during the college's first decade, only fifteen became farmers. The majority of the graduates were employed as teachers, lawyers, and bookkeepers and in other professions.[18]

Thus the curriculum reflected an uneasy compromise between the supporters of a practical education and those of a liberal one. The new college's overall view of itself was nicely illustrated by the images contained in an engraving that appeared on the frontispiece of the school's first catalog. From right to left one first sees a sheaf of grain and a walking plow. Next is a reclining bust of a man resembling George Washington, resting near a scroll. Next to the bust is a laurel wreath and a printed page. The far right-hand corner contains calipers and a large cogged gear. In the center of the engraving is a globe with a telescope behind it. In the background, barely visible behind the other articles, is a cannon.[19]

In spite of the clear language of the Morrill Act, the state legislature's enabling legislation, and the College's vision of itself as a broad-based educational institution, a major gap existed in the institution's operations. The "M" in Mississippi A & M was largely imaginary. In its first biennial appropriation the legislature provided funds to build a 200-man dormitory, a house for the president, and temporary barns and stables, and to purchase 840 acres of farmland. In the next session the legislature provided money to build more dormitories, a hospital, homes for the professors and to purchase equipment "to exemplify varied and diversified agriculture to the best advantage."[20]

The truth was that, although the College's charter stated that it was charged with teaching the "mechanic arts," in practice it had not been permitted to do so. No money, buildings, or equipment had been provided for anything other than liberal and agricultural education. A department of "Mathematics and Engineering" existed, directed by Professor Sullivan; but its curriculum consisted mainly of arithmetic and elementary mathematics, including algebra, plane and spherical geometry, plane trigonometry, and "mensuration and surveying" (probably simple land measurement). "Until shops and conveniences for teaching Mechanics are provided," wrote Sullivan, "it has been thought best to bend the energies of the College to benefit the predominant industry of the State, viz: Agriculture."[21] These things were not immediately forthcoming. Although J. M. Barrow, the new head of the Department of Mathematics, claimed that the department offered a "limited course in Civil Engineering" in 1882, the program existed largely in his imagination, and by 1883 the word engineering had been dropped from the departmental names mentioned in the college catalog. Indeed, the College's entire stock of engineering equipment consisted of a compass, transit, theodolite, plane table, and level.[22] Students inclined to study the "mechanic arts" in a purely intellectual way were no better off than their colleagues who needed equipment. Very few of the periodicals the library received had any bearing on engineering, even when the term is broadly defined. Students interested in the mechanic arts had to content themselves with reading *Carpentry and Building, Drainage and Farm Journal, Manufacturer and Builder, The American Machinist, Oil, Paint and Drug Reporter,* and *The Industrialist.*[23]

Initially, President Lee expressed little interest in the mechanic arts and resisted adding what he called the "mechanical feature" to the Mississippi A & M curriculum. Certainly his dedication to agricultural education explained much of this resistance. Another reason lay with the nature of the Mississippi legislature, during this period a petulant, meddlesome, overbearing body, particularly when it turned its attention to Mississippi A & M. The anti A & M faction in the legislature was led by Frank Burkitt, a leader of the Farmers' Alliance, a group consisting of small farmers whose situation was becoming increasingly desperate during the late nineteenth century. The farmers blamed the A & M College for not making them prosperous immediately. Burkitt had developed a personal and political dislike of President Lee and had forged an anti A & M coalition made up of disgruntled farmers and alumni from the University of Mississippi who were opposed to the goals of the institution and who believed that its success had come at the expense of the university. With this support, Burkitt made it his mission to destroy the new A & M College by, among other things, accusing it of educating "bookfarmers" who believed themselves superior to the man in the field. Very likely, Burkitt and his coalition were displeased by Lee's halting steps to institute a curriculum in mechanics. In 1885 Lee had concluded his biennial report by "respectfully but earnestly asking recognition of the Mechanical feature of the college." The legislature, he wrote, should provide the college with the means to provide instruction in machining wood and metals and in operating steam-operated equipment.[24]

Lee may have been ill-advised to include this request because words such as these greatly irritated people like Burkitt. They suspected that the real goal of President Lee and his faculty had all along been to forget about agriculture as soon as it was politically expedient and to devote their energies to urban-oriented activities.

To a large extent Burkitt's attack paralleled similar attacks on land-grant institutions in other states. The small farmers who made up the membership of the Farmers' Alliance and the Grange had expected the colleges created as a result of the Morrill Act to perform miracles and to lead them into instant prosperity. This had not happened, and the A & M colleges which had aroused such high expectations provided convenient targets for the farmers' wrath.[25]

Burkitt came close to succeeding in his mission. In the 1886-87 biennium he managed to have the state appropriation reduced by over $10,000, and in 1888-89 he engineered a reduction of nearly $15,000. His real purpose was to force reductions in the salaries of the A & M faculty, whom he despised, mainly because they were from the North and were not adequately sympathetic to the needs of the Southern small farmer. Initially Lee and the board of trustees resisted cutting salaries by drawing funds from other accounts, but Burkitt finally triumphed by persuading the legislature to itemize the salaries to be paid to all employees of Mississippi A & M in its appropriation language. The result was a salary reduction of about 25 percent. Enrollment dropped precipitously—from 515 in 1885-86 to 286 in 1887-88, when a wholesale exodus of faculty members took place. Burkitt hailed the departure of these faculty members because he thought it might force the college to hire only Mississippians, who, presumably, would be happy to work for less.[26] Lee must have despaired. During the first three months of the 1888 session two barns, the mess hall, and Lee's own house burned. Convinced that these fires were linked to Burkitt's coalition, Lee saw them as arson, "the culmination of an effort to destroy the institution."[27]

Under these circumstances it is understandable that Lee and the board of trustees hesitated to ask the legislature for money to begin teaching the mechanic arts. Burkitt would have opposed any appropriation that might have detracted from the teaching of practical agriculture. He also would have used such a request as further evidence that the A & M college was not interested in the well-being of Mississippi's farmers. Fear of criticism from populists may also help explain why the mechanic arts program was so unscientific when it was finally introduced into the curriculum in 1892. A low-profile, shop-oriented program would be much less open to attack from such people as Burkitt.

By 1889 the feud with Burkitt had died down and relations with the legislature were much improved. Once again Lee asked the legislature for the funds necessary to teach the mechanic arts. It is not clear why he pursued authorization for the new program so vigorously. He may have been influenced by the fact that few of the College's graduates actually became farmers or that formal agricultural education was not having the dramatic impact on Mississippi agriculture that had been expected by its early proponents.

In addition Lee had become pessimistic about the future of agriculture in the United States. He devoted part of his biennial report for 1889 to a discussion of agriculture's difficulties. Lee had discovered some figures that had alarmed him. In 1860, he noted, farmers comprised half of the country's population and possessed half of the nation's wealth. By 1880 farmers still made up half of the population, but owned only one-fourth of the wealth. When the increases in population and total national wealth were taken into account, Lee went on, agriculture's share had declined by 92 percent. Over half of the nation's farms were fully mortgaged, a figure that may have been much higher in Mississippi.

President Lee also had come to realize that the relationship between agriculture and industry had changed dramatically. Between 1850 to 1860, he observed, agriculture led manufacturing by 10 percent in the value of products, whereas between 1870 and 1880, manufacturing led by 37 percent. Lee had discovered the industrial revolution! Although he ended his report with the curious conclusion that these data proved it was "certainly the duty of the State to foster agricultural education in every way," this may have been simply the old planter in Lee talking, or a Lee that did not wish to further antagonize Mississippians like Burkitt. In truth, the conclusion Lee actually had reached through the development of his argument was a different one: It was clearly time for Mississippi A & M to begin preparing students to enter the new industrial world described by his statistics.[28]

Lee's decision to support the mechanic arts was due in part to the influence of Buz Walker. One of the College's first students, Walker had joined the faculty in 1888 as professor of mathematics. Although he had little to work with in the way of equipment, he was determined to add as much mechanical training to the upper-division curriculum as he could. In the first term of their junior year students were introduced to "the best methods of land, city, trigonometrical, topographical, and mining surveying, leveling, railway curves, and underground traversing." During the next two quarters they studied the "composition, resolution, and equilibrium of forces, rectilinear and periodic, curvilinear and rotary motion, elementary machines, and mechanics of liquids and gases." Seniors studied civil engineering which consisted of studying the adjustment of mathematical instruments, the strength of materials, roof and bridge trusses, railway curves, and excavation and embankments.[29]

Although the legislature did not immediately provide the funds requested, it was more favorably disposed to the A & M college than it had been the year before and it increased the institution's funding. In addition, the Congress passed legislation supplementing the Morrill Act which provided an additional $15,000 to each state to be used for teaching "agriculture, the mechanic arts, the English language and the various branches of mathematical, physical, natural and economic science with special reference to their applications in the industries of life."[30] This sum was to rise by $1,000 each year for ten years until it reached a maximum of $25,000; after that point it was to remain a fixed appropriation. The legislation required states with separate institutions for white and black students to divide the money between them. Ever since the founding of Mississippi A & M College, the money had been divided equally between Mississippi A & M and Alcorn A & M; in 1891, however, the Secretary of the Interior, who had the power to interpret the legislation, forced Mississippi to make a division based on the number of educable children of each race. This meant that Alcorn A & M received 60 percent of the funds. Lee was pleased with the windfall and wrote that it had "fully restored [Mississippi A & M] to its former prosperity and confidence." Although many of the fourteen faculty members who left in 1888 had been replaced with recent A & M graduates, Lee bravely stated that "the faculty is now equal in efficiency and skill to what it was before so many of its number resigned."[31]

Moved by the clear language of the federal legislation of 1890, that specifically required the land-grant colleges to teach much more than agriculture, the college's board of trustees, acting on its own initiative, took the first steps toward establishing a department of mechanic arts. Convinced that the new department could be established with "slight additional expense," Lee somehow had gotten the idea that the U. S. government was prepared to furnish the college with a mechanical engineering professsor in the same way that the army provided an instructor in military science.[32] The board of trustees responded by removing $15,000 from the 1890 and 1891 budgets and designating the funds for starting a mechanic arts department. The college used the initial portion of the money to supplement faculty salaries, purchase a 40 horsepower steam engine and boiler, and buy woodworking and machine tools. In 1891 it spent $2,879 to erect an iron shed 100 by 50 feet which contained the steam engine and boiler. In addition, forty workbenches were installed, which along with several steam-powered saws and lathes, were adequate to serve the woodworking needs of two hundred students. This was a modest beginning, wrote Lee, not adequate to provide degree work in the mechanic arts since it had been "engrafted on the agricultural and horticulture curriculum." The bachelor of science degree in Mechanic arts would come only when the legislature provided buildings and equipment for machine work in iron and for forge and foundry work, "so that practical manual training can accompany theoretical instruction in all the usual divisions of a mechanic arts course." Members of the legislature were enthusiastically informed that as a result of the assistance from Congress, the college had "taken on new life . . . as the mechanical feature has been started."[33]

Sixty-five students appeared in September 1891 for instruction in the mechanic arts. Their drawing facilities were ready, but due to the slowness of suppliers, the college could not complete the woodworking shop until November. Delivery problems were not the only things hampering the inauguration of the mechanic arts department. No serious attempt had ever been made to offer such a program in Mississippi before. As a result, many students had no clear idea of what was expected of them. Also, some of the classically oriented faculty were cool to the new program. Nevertheless, the legislature was impressed by Congress's specific language and by the college's preliminary work, and in 1892 it appropriated $10,000 for the mechanic arts program which Lee, Buz Walker and Harry Gwinner (the new Superintendent of the Mechanical Department) used to build and equip a tiny (35 by 70 feet) metalworking shop. Initially Gwinner had envisioned a two-story iron building with drawing facilities on the second floor and the metal shop on the first floor. But the legislature had not provided adequate funding, and he had to settle for a one-story metal shed with an earthen floor. Twelve students could study blacksmithing and foundry work at the same time, and up to eight could study metal machining. After fourteen years the "mechanical feature" had become a permanent part of Mississippi A & M College.[34]

Instruction in the mechanic arts at Mississippi A & M was at first modest, reflecting both the paucity of resources and equipment and the shop-oriented philosophy of the department. Nestled among the usual required freshman courses were three new courses: Elements of Mechanism, Workshop Methods, and Shop Work, which included carpentry, pattern making, and molding. Sophomores took two quarters of drawing and in the afternoons studied shop work, blacksmithing, and machining. As usual juniors learned the techniques of surveying in the first quarter, but began studying mechanics and electricity and magnetism in the second quarter. When mechanic arts students became seniors they took additional drawing and several specialized courses in mechanics. The second term of the senior year included analytical mechanics; strength of materials and engineering, steam engines, and machine drawing, and the third term included additional machine designing, steam boilers, and mechanical engineering. Afternoons were still devoted to shop and laboratory work. Even a graduate program in the mechanic arts had been established. In theory graduate students could pursue advanced study in such areas as the design of steam plants, engineering structures, hydraulics, and steam and water heating.35

Because the educational philosophy of the new department was not yet clearly focused, it reflected the conflicts inherent in providing an urban-oriented program in one of the most rural, least industrialized states in the nation. This philosophy also reflected the conflict between engineering educators who believed that students should be taught primarily shop techniques and those who wished to prepare liberally educated professionals. Thus prospective students were told that the mechanical course was designed to allow them to "continue the elementary, scientific, and literary studies, together with free hand and mechanical drawing, while receiving theoretical and practical instruction in the various mechanic arts." They would not be taught to use a single set of faculties, "but to develop harmoniously all the powers . . . on the principle that the eye and hand should be educated no less than the brain." This promise to the students put the college in a quandary. The facilities and equipment obtained under the new program were essentially those useful for teaching shop techniques. Although this fit in with Lee's obsession with practicality, the faculty did not want their program to be known simply as a training shop for carpenters and blacksmiths. As a compromise, Lee and the faculty decided that they would not try to teach the trades but would teach the principles and processes underlying them. Lee hoped that such an approach would allow students to quickly "get wages beyond those of a journeyman," and "aspire to a foremanship or superintendency of manufacturing enterprises." This was to be accomplished by providing the students with a series of lessons that would teach them the principles underlying ordinary tools, machines, and practices of carpentry and iron work. The goal was "to cover all the essential principles, in the various Mechanic Arts, and acquire fair skill of hand and eye, and develop fully the observing and perceptive faculties of the mind." This instruction was intended to prepare students to fill important positions in Mississippi and thus make it unnecessary for the state to import mechanics and workmen from other states.[36]

Lee and Walker drew up a list of equipment needed to teach the principles of mechanics. A glance at the list illustrates the kind of training Lee wanted to give the advanced students. Essentially, Lee wanted students to learn by observing models that would provide "object lessons" which could then be used to teach first principles. Devices with moving parts were necessary, and Lee requested funds to purchase a set from Germany. The set included a machine designed to illustrate "the parallelogram of forces," a bent lever, an inclined plane, a screw, an endless screw, and a device illustrating the laws of the wedge. The other equipment desired was similar in nature including such things as windlasses, blocks and pulleys, and a crank handle and axle.[37]

During the 1892-93 session 122 students received instruction in the mechanic arts and Harry Gwinner, superintendent of the mechanical department and instructor in drawing, made a valiant effort to combine the theoretical and the practical. Classes were offered in bench work, carpentry and woodworking, patternmaking, foundry work, and blacksmithing. Students learned to manage a forge, make castings, and shape and machine metal. Then they fabricated a tool or a piece of machinery which allowed them to demonstrate their shop skills. The products were not very advanced—in 1892-93 students using a forge made several pairs of blacksmith tongs, a few machine tools, and the ironwork for a plow.[38]

Shop work was complemented by theoretical work in mathematics, design, and drawing. Freshman studied commercial arithmetic, bookkeeping and banking, and college algebra. Sophomores studied plane geometry, solid geometry, trigonometry, and a special course called descriptive geometry during the third quarter. Juniors took surveying and analytic geometry during the first quarter and differential calculus and integral calculus during the second and third quarters. During the second and third terms students also took analytic geometry and mechanics, a course where mathematical principles were applied to everyday mechanics. Seniors studied strength of materials and analytic mechanics during the first quarter and civil engineering during the second. They ended their theoretical studies by taking a quarter of astronomy. Drawing students learned basic lettering and shading and projections, which they applied to drawing machine parts. Their final task was to draw a monkey wrench and its component parts.[39]

Gwinner initially required one sophomore student per week to work in the engine house and help tend the engine and boiler, an exercise he considered "of the utmost importance to students learning the engineering branch." Even though the college operated under a system of military discipline, and entering students had been informed that "the military feature is the most effective means of enforcing and securing discipline," students rebelled at being forced to work as unpaid steam engine and boiler attendants, and lack of cooperation forced Gwinner to abandon this requirement after four or five weeks. He thought that President Lee should require the students to work as boiler and engine room assistants. Gwinner's comments on the issue illustrate the kind of occupations he expected students in the new program to follow. "How is a student ever to learn the erection of engines and boilers in gin houses, saw and grist mills if he does not get some ideas on these points?" he wrote.[40]

The faculty worked closely with the first mechanic arts students and their descriptions of their students' work during the first two years of the college's existence are timeless. At first the students did not understand what the shop was really for, and "some of them suppose[d that] the shop was a sort of playroom and it required some little time to teach them that shop work was as of much importance as the knowledge obtained for their textbooks." Some thought that learning to use the saw, hammer, and plane was degrading and Gwinner complained of the "slowness of the students in comprehending the true value of the work." Drawing bored them; they saw little value in it and "slighted it as much as possible" because it did not "possess the fascination that shop work does." Nineteenth-century engineering educators viewed drawing as the one essential skill that bound the rest of the curriculum together, and the faculty found this attitude inexcusable.[41]

Many of the students probably had never seen the inside of a machine shop before and teaching them to respect the machinery was often a difficult task. Gwinner had to defend one of his instructors from students who resented him because of his bluntness with them. Such treatment was necessary, Gwinner thought, because the "students at times handle machines they have no business with . . . . and to keep them from getting hurt one is compelled to speak quickly." The students liked to play with the gears on the machines, ignoring warnings to stop. Some day, Gwinner worried, "some of them are going to miss some fingers and we will receive the blame for not telling them."[42]

Housing for the fledgling department was primitive. During the first session the carpenter shop could not be heated because it was only a shell with no interior walls. The blacksmith shop and foundry were lined partly with sheet iron to keep sparks from igniting the woodwork. Screens were placed over the shop windows to prevent the glass from being broken and give the buildings an appearance of security. Drainage tiles were installed around the machine shop to keep water from seeping around the machinery.[43]

The students and faculty persevered, and in 1895 the bachelor of science degree was awarded to eight seniors. Among the eight graduates were two outstanding students who later became leaders of the institution: D. C. Hull and Randle Churchill Carpenter. Hull served as president of Mississippi A & M from 1920 to 1925 and Carpenter served as professor of mechanical and electrical engineering and Dean of the School of Engineering from 1930 to 1938.[44] In his 1893 report to President Lee, Professor Gwinner had commended Carpenter and Hull for their excellence in drawing and praised Carpenter for his blacksmithing abilities.[45]

Gwinner found the challenge of administering a mechanic arts department on a shoestring overwhelming, however, and in 1894 resigned to take a similar post at the University of Maryland. His successor was A. J. Weichardt, a man of seemingly unlimited energy whose understanding of the mechanic arts was much broader than Gwinner's. In his first report to President Lee, Weichardt made several wide-ranging recommendations which ultimately shaped the development of the college in this century. Apparently Weichardt had deduced that, from the college's earliest years, the letters A & M really meant "general purpose college" to almost everyone involved with the institution except for President Lee and such people as Frank Burkitt. Even though Weichardt acknowledged that the term mechanic arts usually referred to wood and iron work at A & M colleges, he thought that Mississippi A & M could easily expand the meaning of the term to include the "art of cotton manufacture" and recommended that the college begin formal instruction in cotton finishing as soon as possible. He also urged the college to begin the study of electricity and establish laboratories where construction materials and machines could be evaluated and tested. Weichardt made these recommendations more palatable to the practical-minded Lee by urging the establishment of a program of two-year courses for shop-oriented students that would teach the trades of carpentry, blacksmithing, foundry work, and metal machining. Such a course would be attractive to "students having but a short time to prepare themselves for future occupations." In addition Weichardt recommended revising the curriculum to better distinguish it from agriculture, adding the study of electricity and reducing the amount of woodworking. Finally, he sought to further separate the mechanic arts program from agriculture by conferring a new degree, the bachelor of mechanical engineering.[46]

Lee respected Weichardt's ideas. In his biennial report for 1894-96 he included a forceful request for the establishment of an electrical program. Lee began his request in an odd manner for the president of a college in one of the country's most rural states. Electrical studies were important, he told the Board, because of the growing importance of electrical propulsion in the streetcar industry. In a more relevant vein he then told the board how valuable electricity was for lighting, heating, cooking, and welding, and that he believed it was destined to become one of the great industries. Yet Mississippi possessed no means of providing instruction in electricity.

Lee saved his most persuasive idea for last. Using an argument that would become familiar to his successors, he told the trustees that the instructional program in electricity could be started at little or no cost since the same buildings and equipment could be used for both instruction and as a source of power for the campus. After all, he said, students were required to purchase both kerosene and lamps to burn it in, which cost them $1,200 per year. This was not only expensive, it was dangerous as well. "In the hands of careless boys using kerosene," Lee wrote, "great danger is incurred to the public property." For an investment of $15,000 in an electrical plant, a cost that would soon be recovered by savings in kerosene, the campus could be lit and an electrical laboratory provided for instruction.[47]

Although the legislature ignored Lee's requests at first, he kept repeating them, and by 1897 a course in electrical engineering was being taught to the senior class. Seniors were taught the basic principles of dynamos, transformers, motors, secondary batteries, and lamps, as well as how to install electrical generating plants. In 1899, the name of the program was changed to "Mechanic Arts and Electricity."[48]

By the turn of the century the mechanic arts curriculum had become more theoretical and less oriented toward the trades. Although the freshman year still consisted mainly of shop work, entering students had begun the study of algebra and mechanical drawing. The sophistication of entering students had improved to such an extent that elementary arithmetic no longer had to be taught during the freshman year. Sophomores studied physics, which in 1898 had been moved to the Mechanic Arts Department from Chemistry, and took introductory classes in the principles of mechanics, heat, electricity and magnetism, and sound and light. Juniors studied Graphic Statics which was a course in basic stress analysis, and learned to build and install steam boilers. Seniors studied the same topics at a more advanced level and prepared working models of machines.[49]

What the college called "laboratory work" had begun as well, although the work consisted entirely of required hours in the various plants that served the college. Electrical engineering students helped operate the new lighting plant built by Weichardt and his students during the summer of 1898.[50] The plant contained a direct-current generator connected to a high-speed compound steam engine—which supplied current for arc lamps, and incandescent lamps—and a ten horsepower motor used to power the machines in the woodworking shop. Mechanical engineering students learned to fire the boilers and operate the college's electric light plant, air compressors, and pumps. Equipment purchased for the new textile school enabled the college to provide additional opportunities for mechanic arts students to learn the basics of operating a steam plant. A new frame boiler-house contained two 125-horsepower return tubular boilers for supplying steam to the Textile Department, the laundry, the mess hall, the chemical laboratory, students' dormitories, and power for the waterworks, electric lights, and shops.[51]

Professor Weichardt was an energetic man and willing to use his electrical and mechanical training to develop the college's physical plant. In 1898 he had devoted his summer vacation to overseeing the installation of the new electricity generating machinery. And in 1897-1898 he, Buz Walker, and their students recased the campus well, installed an air compressor as part of the campus water-distribution system, and designed and erected a hundred-foot iron water tower with a 30,000-gallon tank. They laid almost two miles of two-and three-inch water mains with thirty fire plugs and installed twelve hundred feet of two–inch pipe in campus buildings. President Lee was proud of the accomplishments of the Mechanic Arts faculty and congratulated them for saving the college a considerable sum of money. By performing this work in addition to their regular duties in the classrooms and shops, Weichardt and Walker set a precedent followed by their successors. Until the establishment of a separate department of campus utilities in 1938, the professors of mechanical and electrical engineering were responsible for supervising all aspects of the physical plant.[52]

Lee resigned the presidency of Mississippi A & M College in May 1899, leaving behind an institution considerably different from the college envisioned in 1878. Instead of a tiny college concentrating on agriculture, Mississippi A & M had become a multipurpose institution providing students with a broad education, which included the opportunity to gain experience in agriculture or mechanics. Mississippians, Lee believed, were pleased with the work of an institution that provided their children with "a thoroughly practical education." Furthermore, he wrote, "A large class of our people desire the young men of the State to combine manual labor and laboratory work with literary instruction. . . ." Lee was especially proud of the mechanic arts program, which provided "very important instruction to the citizens of Mississippi in the great progress now going on." Indeed, by 1899, 55 percent of the male students in the junior class were choosing the mechanical courses.[53]

Lee and his faculty had fought many battles and overcome many obstacles during the years 1878-1899. Some of the battles were won and some lost, but there was no longer any question about the future viability of the institution and its "mechanical feature." Though possessing inadequate resources, Lee had fought with great courage. In many ways he had done exactly what a retired Confederate general was prepared to do: struggle against adversaries that were often unseen and unsuspected. He and his faculty had often retreated, but had never surrendered. In many ways Lee's experience provided a paradigm for the institution as it moved into the twentieth century.

CHAPTER TWO

The Challenges of Growth

Stephen D. Lee was succeeded by John M. Stone, a former governor of Mississippi who had been an early, staunch supporter of Mississippi A & M College. Stone was not a young man when he assumed leadership of the institution, and he died the following March.

The board selected as his successor John Crumpton Hardy. Hardy was an ambitious, vigorous man of thirty-six whose understanding of Mississippi's higher and secondary education was broad. A native of Newton, Mississippi, Hardy, unlike his predecessors, had not been shaped by the experience of Reconstruction. His education included stays at Mississippi College, Millsaps College, the University of Chicago, and Cornell. Initially, Hardy had hoped to become a lawyer and had taken a teaching post in order to support himself during his law studies. Teaching agreed with him, and he began a career in education that eventually led to the superintendency of the Jackson public schools. He was brash, supremely confident of himself, and certain that no obstacle could prevent him from achieving his goal of turning Mississippi A & M College into an institution respected throughout the South.[1]

The institution over which Hardy was to preside for twelve years was a modest one. The academic building, a dormitory, and the chemical laboratories formed the heart of the campus. Around them were clustered a handful of faculty residences, barns, and utility buildings. (None of these buildings now exists.) Ten departments employed thirty staff members who taught some 300 students a year. Hardy's arrival coincided with a period of unprecedented expansion, as 516 students arrived for the 1900-1901 session.[2]

Hardy, who had lived in the North long enough to understand the central role that industry was to play in the economy of the twentieth century, was not obsessed with the Southern agrarian tradition. Having decided to emphasize mechanical and industrial education, in 1902 he recommended that the existing curriculum in Mechanic Arts be transformed into a school of engineering. He was enthusiastically supported in this project by faculty members from Mechanic Arts. One of Hardy's most ardent supporters was Charles Edgar Ard, who had been employed as an adjunct professor of mechanic arts and electricity in 1901. Ard believed strongly that the future of Mississippi lay in its ability to industrialize. He believed that the entire economic plight of the South, with its loss of intellectual and financial supremacy, could be traced to the weaknesses of Southern higher education. Ard thought higher education in Mississippi was especially deficient because it was oriented too heavily toward "literary pursuit" and was incapable of producing an adequate supply of technically oriented people who knew how to add value to the raw materials produced in Mississippi. Cattle, for example, left Mississippi for St. Louis where every ounce of weight, even the hair of the animal, was converted into a product that did not further increase in value. The same was true of cotton, logs, and vegetables, all of which could be increased in value by combining "technically trained intelligence and manually trained labor." A school of engineering could remedy this unfortunate situation, Ard thought, by providing technological education that would "more quickly bring results than any other method."[3]

Buz Walker—an early graduate of the Mechanic Arts Department who had returned to Mississippi A & M College in 1900 to head the Mathematics Department after completing course work for his Ph.D. degree at the University of Chicago—also vigorously supported Hardy's plan to establish a school of engineering. Like Ard, Walker believed that Mississippi A & M engineers could create a great industrial future for the state. In the future, Walker wrote, Mississippi's engineers would be called upon to develop the state's oil industry, build new roads, explore the geological structure of soils, and direct the exploitation of timber resources. It was clearly the responsibility of the college to train "Mississippi boys . . . [to] take the lead in the development of any industrial enterprise that may be carried on with profit in the state." Whereas Ard thought the new school of engineering should confine itself to teaching the "basic principles underlying technical education," and not try to compete with the great technical universities, Walker believed that Mississippi A & M College could soon be the equal of the leading universities in the United States. Instead of following Ard's recommendation to provide only a kind of advanced manual training, Walker wanted to give students a good general education, a mastery of the fundamental principles of mathematics, and an understanding of the scientific principles that underlay the engineering professions.[4]

On June 3, 1902, the board of trustees formally established the new school. Hardy completed the reorganization of the college by creating a school of agriculture, which was later joined by a textile school. In his report to President Hardy in 1902, Walker had modestly left a blank where the name of the new school's director should have gone. This was somewhat disingenuous: Walker was immediately appointed the first director of the School of Engineering and later became its first dean.[5]

Throughout the state's history Mississippians have alternated between periods of looking outward for sources of inspiration and support and periods marked by introspection, withdrawal, and suspicion of the outside world. The periods of extroversion were often accompanied by enthusiasm for education, particularly the kind of education that would allow the state and its residents to take better advantage of what the industrial world has to offer. The periods of introspection, on the other hand, have been characterized by a xenophobia that has as its main feature anti-intellectualism and suspicion of any kind of education that questions the traditional political, social, and religious values of Mississippians.

The early years of this century were years of extroversion, and the inauguration of Governor Andrew H. Longino in January 1900 marked the beginning of the period. Longino was the first post-Civil War governor of Mississippi who had not served in the Confederate Army. He was a man who believed that if Mississippi were ever to improve its social and economic position it would have to overcome its traditional suspicion of the industrialized North and of the Northern businesses and corporations that were its principal engines. Longino believed that technical education was an important key to promoting industrial development and in his inaugural address asked the legislature to support technologically oriented education. Partly because of his leadership and partly because of the slightly improved economic conditions of the state, the legislature passed several pieces of legislation promoting technical education during the next few years.[6]

In 1900, the legislature appropriated $40,000 for the construction of a new textile school at Mississippi A & M. This appropriation inspired hope among the mechanic arts faculty that a new building could be built for the School of Engineering (the old foundry had burned in March, 1902). In his final report, Professor Weichardt had recommended building a much larger brick building for the forge and foundry and erecting a second building for the college's steam machinery. The faculty must have received considerable encouragement from President Hardy: all their projections and descriptions of needs were based on the assumption that a new building for engineering would be forthcoming, which would be "commensurate with the importance of the work."[7]

Their optimism was not misplaced, and in 1904 construction began on a new engineering building, with Professors Ard and Albert Barnes, Head of Mechanical Engineering, acting as construction superintendents. Contractors submitted bids that ranged between $37,000 and $46,000. Ard and Barnes, using students as laborers, completed the work for $30,000.

The resulting building was made of pressed brick, which was finished with stone. The three-story main part, extending east and west, was 60 by 122 feet. Three wings extended from it. The first floor of the main building was used by the Department of Mechanical Engineering as a classroom, laboratory, and machine shop. Civil Engineering and Drawing occupied the second floor, and the third floor was used for storage. The west wing contained the forge and foundry. The east wing housed the power and light plants and the south wing contained an office for the Department of Mechanical Engineering, a workroom and office for the Department of Physics and Electrical Engineering. "The facilities, convenience, and arrangement," boasted the 1905-06 catalog, "are unsurpassed."[8]

What the catalog told prospective students, however, was something other than the complete truth. In actuality, the building was inadequate almost from the day it was first occupied. When the building was designed, only the Mechanic Arts Department existed, although the faculty expected other departments to be added soon. Thus, when the building was erected, Ard and Barnes tried to increase the size of the rooms as much as they could while staying within the appropriation intended solely for the Mechanic Arts Department. Indeed, by 1907, the original Mechanic Arts Department had evolved into the departments of Mechanical, Civil, Electrical, and Geology and Mining Engineering. When the building was designed there were around a dozen students in the upper classes. By 1907, the faculty was teaching sixty-six students in the upper-level classes, in addition to the numerous freshmen and sophomores who took the basic courses. Although the building had never been intended to include the Physics Department, the department was housed there for lack of other space. Physics suffered from this arrangement because the engineering departments used heavy steam and electrical equipment in their laboratories and the vibrations set up by this machinery made it difficult to perform delicate demonstrations and experiments. Laboratory space was so limited that different classes had to use the same rooms, which meant that apparatus had to be disassembled and reassembled between laboratory sessions.[9]

Raiding space occupied by other academic departments is not unusual in underequipped institutions. Even the mild-mannered Barnes felt compelled to fight for space at the expense of another. In 1907, he wrote to President Hardy, bypassing Walker, asking Hardy to evict a professor of rural engineering from a groundfloor room where he was storing farm machinery. Barnes needed the room for a new program in manual training for women. New and different workshop benches had to be installed in the room for them. The existing benches were not suitable because they were not built with sufficient leg space underneath. "We can hardly expect the ladies who will take this work," Barnes wrote, "to remain standing for hours." He concluded his request for more space by offering the president a kind of bribe. Instead of taking the vacation Hardy had granted him, Barnes offered to stay on campus so he could reline the shafts in the machine shop and reset and adjust his machine tools.[10]

The state legislature's newfound enthusiasm for technical education buoyed the spirits of the engineering faculty, leading them to believe it might finally be possible to acquire adequate equipment, which would allow them to familiarize their students with the kind of machines normally found in industry. Before 1904, only the forge and the drawing room were properly equipped. Because the wood shop contained no industrial equipment, most students completed their courses in woodworking using only hand tools. In order to provide industrial-level instruction, wrote Barnes to the president, the department needed a sander, planer, and surfacer, as well as a machine for making mortises and tenons, and a drying kiln. The machine shop also needed a milling machine, gear cutter, and drill press. The new engineering laboratory existed in name only, as its equipment was "practically nothing," consisting almost entirely of the machines that supplied the campus with steam and electricity. The electrical engineering laboratory lacked the most basic equipment and machinery that students would normally encounter in the production and transmission of electricity. Barnes had long wanted to teach students the basics of commercial icemaking but had failed to obtain funding. He finally realized that the surest way to get his new equipment was to make it part of the campus system of utilities. He received the equipment after he pointed out that it would pay for itself by supplying the refrigeration needs of the dairy and farms and would generate income through sales to individuals.[11]

Even the new Textile Building became a part of the engineering laboratory system. It had quickly become clear that the architects had made a serious mistake when choosing a source of power for the machines. Initially the textile equipment was operated by the line-shaft system of power transmission (the standard in the nineteenth century). A line-shaft power-transmission system consisted of a long overhead drive shaft connected by a belt to a steam engine located at one end of the shaft. Large pulleys on the shaft transmitted power to machines by means of wide, flat leather belts. Inefficient, dangerous, noisy, and dirty, line-shaft installations also required constant lubrication and repair. On Ard's recommendation the Textile School replaced the line-shaft system with electric motors that could be used to train students in electrical-power transmission.[12]

The curriculum of the School of Engineering became more professional and theoretical, not quite as dependent on the acquisition of shop skills as the Mechanic Arts curriculum had been. Indeed, the school began to reflect the kind of academic tension that was to mark it and the engineering profession in general during the twentieth century. The essential argument was between those who wanted students to develop skills that could immediately be applied on the job and those who wanted to train broadly educated students whose knowledge of athematics, science, and society would enable them to move easily in professional circles. The development of the curriculum during the early years of the School of Engineering illustrates this disagreement. Buz Walker, the first director of the school, was a mathematician, not an engineer, and he had a philosophy of engineering which was more theoretical than the one held by his predecessors in the mechanic arts. As Walker saw it, the primary object of his school was to train students "in those fundamental principles of mathematics and along the different lines of engineering work which make the foundation and form the basis of all successful specialization." All training was bound together by drawing, the "universal language of the engineer" and the main medium for the transmission of engineering ideas. Besides performing their teaching and campus duties, the faculty were to "help citizens and others by giving information, recommending competent men to fill positions in engineering work, and assisting in the solution of engineering problems of interest to the State."[13]

Albert Barnes thought that no student should graduate from the college without thorough training in mechanics, which he considered necessary for the future industrialization of the state. Labor was becoming increasingly scarce, he wrote. "Machinery and labor-saving devices are playing such a role in the farm and plantation life of the progressive agriculturalist, that no student in the Agricultural department should be graduated from this College until he has a general working knowledge of steam boilers, steam engines, gasoline engines, pumps, windmills, and hydraulic rams, that may be of service to him in his chosen field." With loggers busy clearing the last of Mississippi's virgin forests, Barnes foresaw the importance of learning to finish forest products. If the state was willing to install expensive machines "to teach the methods of working up the cotton crop into cloth and thereby increasing the value of the cotton industry," it should also be willing to purchase "machinery to work up timber and teach methods of converting cheap lumber into high-priced building material, furniture, and articles of commerce."[14]

Ard and Barnes won this argument, and the curriculum retained much of the practical focus it had maintained since the founding of the college. In the mechanical engineering curriculum, for example, woodworking and blacksmithing continued as the basis for engineering education during the students' freshman and sophomore years. During the first term of the freshman year students studied woodworking for two hours per week, which prepared them for more extensive work in the second and third terms. During those semesters more advanced wood-shop training was required, in which students learned the basics of cutting, gluing, dovetailing, and framing. They also made simple shaped articles with saws, planes, and lathes. In the sophomore year students took two hours of woodworking each term and learned to construct simple furniture. They also began forge work, which involved the building of forge fires and bending and welding iron. Juniors continued with shop, foundry, and machine-shop work and began the study of mechanical engineering. They studied elementary mechanics and learned to assemble and repair steam boilers and engines.

About the only indication that the curriculum had become more scientific was the introduction to the junior curriculum of a course called "kinematics." The subjects covered by these courses included the transmission of power by belts, ropes, and shafting, the design of cams and gears, and the study of various engines and boilers. Seniors were introduced to gas engines and high-speed steam engines, icemaking and refrigeration, and air compressors. Barnes required both seniors and juniors to dismantle, reassemble, and operate steam boilers and engines and learn to operate the equipment installed in the college powerhouse. Their college years culminated in the construction of a "graduating piece"—a special machine tool designed to illustrate the student's skill as a machinist.[15]

Ard's electrical engineering students followed a highly practical course of study. Most of their work involved studying the production, transmission, and consumption of electricity; they learned little about the theory of the form of energy that was transforming Europe and the United States. Other than the machines available in the campus power plant, the department's equipment consisted of a darkroom designed to perform efficiency tests on different sources of electric light, a dynamo laboratory with fifteen different generators and alternators, and various transformers and meters. Juniors concentrated on the generation and distribution of direct current. They studied the construction of electrical switchboards, line construction, and the operation of direct current-power systems. Seniors studied the production, transmission, and use of alternating current. In addition, the department was directly responsible for providing college buildings with electrical power. The faculty and students operated the 115-kilowatt-hour generators which provided current to 1500 lights and 18 motors.[16]

Civil Engineering, which had been part of the agricultural curriculum since the earliest years of the college, became part of the School of Engineering in September 1902. Rural Engineering (which became Agricultural Engineering in 1910) continued to meet the needs of students in agriculture who studied such things as ditching, terracing, and draining land. The main concern of the new Civil Engineering Department was instruction in the techniques of building dirt roads, something Hardy thought essential to the future prosperity of the state. The earliest civil engineering students concentrated on this aspect of their craft by studying surveying, leveling, roadbed construction, and the building of bridges.

Although the *Bulletin* for 1904 promised students in Civil Engineering that they would be able to study such subjects as Theoretical Hydraulics and Water Supply Engineering, training in these areas was rudimentary at best. Most of this ambitious curriculum was beyond the capability of the School of Engineering; the Civil Engineering Department possessed virtually no equipment. In all, the department had two transits, one theodolite, one Y level, one dumpy level, one plane table, two compasses, and assorted rods, tapes, and chains. In truth, the first students spent most of their time completing different tasks around the college grounds. For instance, the first juniors made a topographical survey of the college. They started at the Illinois Central depot, where the elevation above sea level was known, and proceeded to chart elevations of the surrounding area. They also worked at laying sewer lines, grading land, digging hillside ditches, and placing irrigation pipes. Seniors did take one term of railway engineering, one term of hydraulic engineering, and one term of sewerage and tile drainage.[17]

The sympathy for industrialization that accompanied the inauguration of Governor Longino was short-lived, and Mississippi politicians soon resumed their attacks on industry. The renewed attacks were familiar ones and came from agricultural interests disappointed with the college's inability to bring immediate prosperity to Mississippi's agriculture. One critic added the state and federal appropriations to the fees charged students and concluded that the college was spending almost $300 per year per student. Most of this money had been wasted, he thought, because President Hardy could provide him only with the names of ninety-five graduates actually engaged in agriculture of which seventeen were employed by Mississippi A & M and twenty-four by other educational institutions. Thus, in twenty-eight years only fifty-four of the ninety-five were engaged in practical agricultural. "I submit," he wrote, "that the making of scientific farmers of the intensive variety at the A. & M. College is a very costly experience."[18] To Mississippians of like minds engineering education was clearly irrelevant. The sad experience of the Textile School illustrates the tendency of Mississippians in the early part of this century to turn their backs on industry. Although the Textile School moved into its handsome building in 1904 with much fanfare, it was never properly staffed or equipped; after nine years of slow starvation, it closed.

The School of Engineering also found itself fighting for its life against politicians who viewed technical education as part of a Northern plot to destroy Mississippi's way of life. Longino was succeeded by James K. Vardaman, a race-baiting populist who opposed Longino's efforts to entice industry to the state through tax exemptions and promised to oppose increased appropriations to the state's colleges in his inaugural address.[19] Thus the School of Engineering was constantly on the defensive and searching for ways to justify its educational program to the people of the state.

Part of the school's poor image among Mississippi politicians stemmed from its placement record. While the school rarely had difficulty in finding jobs for its graduates, most were employed by firms outside Mississippi. Although mechanical engineering graduates who wished to remain in Mississippi could find employment operating cotton gins, sawmills, and ice plants, practically the only jobs to be found within the state that were suitable for electrical engineering graduates were in municipal power plants. In general, graduates did not stay long in these positions because the technology then in use was usually primitive and salaries were extremely low. Students tended to use these positions simply to gain experience, then moved to more satisfying and better-paying positions.

Under these circumstances, improving the ability of the School of Engineering to serve Mississippi was a daunting task. Even though Mississippi was extremely rural, the engineering faculty fervently believed that the state's future would be shaped by the level of industrialization Mississippi achieved, which, in turn, was connected to the number of technically trained men employed within its borders. Yet, graduates with engineering degrees either could not find employment within the state or would not accept it, primarily because local people did not appreciate the value of their training.

The conditions prevailing in Mississippi's municipal power plants illustrates the conflict which then existed between faculty of the School of Engineering (who were committed to technical education) and local industrial attitudes and practices. Mississippi's power plants were operated in slipshod fashion, and their managers and employees were often hired for reasons other than their technical ability. Ard complained constantly about the incompetence of the operators of municipal power plants, men who knew little about common business practices and who refused to offer salaries adequate to attract trained engineers. Two of the most progressive towns in the state, he noted, had recently hired Mississippi A & M students as superintendents of power plants, neither of whom had been able to pass from the Preparatory Department to the college even after several years of effort. Ard considered these young men, probably hired for political reasons, typical of power-plant superintendents in the state; neither young man was bright enough to determine the cost of the power produced or to understand the operating principles of the machinery in use. As a result of such hiring practices, municipal power plants had to rely on equipment salesmen to advise them about purchases. These salesmen had managed to fill Mississippi's power plants with obsolete equipment their companies wanted to dump. Ard had spent considerable effort trying to convince plant managers in the state to employ more graduates at better salaries, but he failed. In 1909, he gave up trying to find in-state employment for electrical engineering graduates and informed President Hardy that he had been encouraging the "men of the past few classes to go to the large manufacturing companies against a better judgement which dictated supplying first the men who were needed in the state."[20]

Even though he had given up hope that Mississippi industries would ever pay well enough to attract graduates in electrical engineering, Ard could not bring himself to turn his back totally on the goal of industrializing the state. In spite of its negative political climate the state required skilled men. The solution, Ard thought, was to establish a new program that would fill the gap. Mississippi A & M, he told President Hardy, should begin to educate brick and stonemasons, carpenters, tinners, plumbers, wiremen, and other skilled workers. "The statistics of this Institution and of any town in the State," he went on, "would indicate far more need for artisans than for professional men." If this type of training were available, "we would mislead fewer young men into attractive higher courses and thus ruin a good artisan."[21]

Thus the pressure was on for Mississippi A & M—and particularly the School of Engineering, which exported almost all of its graduates—to justify itself to the people of the state. One possibility, thought Ard, was for the members of the engineering faculty to initiate an engineering extension service similar to agricultural extension. "The popular mind," he wrote, "is rapidly becoming clear of the impression that a college professor is incompetent in a practical way." The status of the institution could be enhanced by having the department heads go out into the state and advise state industries. If a way could be devised to make the school responsible for training and licensing operating engineers, Mississippi A & M would soon have complete control of industrial work in the state, especially of power plants and railways. Among Ard's suggestions were the expansion of campus services for demonstration purposes. The college could begin to operate a telephone exchange of its own, as well as a printing plant, and could promote the construction of an electric railway from the college to Starkville so that students could learn to work with that technology. Ard viewed electric railways as almost magical in their ability to transform rural areas by modernizing small towns and agricultural communities. The Gulf Coast and Delta regions were ready for electric railways, which had the ability to "rapidly develop industry in any section."[22]

Ard's suggestions for increasing the scope and responsibility of the School of Engineering reflected the enthusiasm and dynamism of President Hardy, who was leading Mississippi A & M through a period of dramatic expansion. Such growth and change inevitably caused friction with the faculty. Hardy's personality was not a conciliatory one; the aggressiveness and stubbornness that led him to preside over the transformation of Mississippi A & M from a tiny training school to a true college were also characteristics that many found irritating. During his tenure as president he antagonized nearly all the constituent groups that make up a college or university, including the students, faculty, and alumni.[23]

In 1908, members of the Alumni Association circulated petitions accusing Hardy of nebulous misdemeanors, including making misstatements to the people of Mississippi, having lax methods and an overbearing attitude, being a millstone around the neck of the college, and conducting himself in a way "unbecoming an officer and a gentlemen." Although the board of trustees rejected these charges after interviewing nearly all of the faculty, Hardy never regained his earlier standing among the faculty and students. The demoralized condition of the student body and the college community had made instruction difficult, wrote Charles Hancock, professor of Drawing and Civil Engineering, as students were marked by a "lack of zeal and interest." They would not even attend baseball games, although Hardy had canceled classes for the purpose. His standing with the faculty plummeted as well because of his practice of summarily firing those who disagreed with him. In spite of warm commendations from Walker, Hardy fired Albert Barnes in 1910, probably with the encouragement of Professor Ard, who quickly moved from head of electrical engineering to head of mechanical engineering.[24]

The main element in Hardy's ability to overcome his opponents among the faculty, students, and alumni, was the support of the Governor of Mississippi, Edmund F. Noel. When Earl Brewer succeeded Noel in 1912, Hardy promptly resigned. He could not resist taking one last parting shot at the faculty, however. It would be the proper course, Hardy wrote in his letter of resignation, for all the members of the faculty to resign along with him as a group so that the board of trustees could retain or reject faculty members as it wished.[25]

Although Hardy left Mississippi A & M under some pressure, he left behind an institution significantly better than when he arrived. In his letter of resignation he noted that when he had been placed in charge of Mississippi A & M in April 1900, fewer than 300 students attended the college. In February 1912, when he left, there were 1,200. His most important legacy, he believed, was the building of "a community based on the aristocracy of efficiency." In what was perhaps a reply to his detractors—who thought that all nontechnical curricula should be located at the University of Mississippi—Hardy noted that "the aristocracy of blood, the aristocracy of wealth, and the aristocracy of learning have all been superseded by the aristocracy of efficiency, in which every boy is measured by what he is and what he can do."[26]

The School of Engineering was perhaps Hardy's most important legacy. Not only had it survived the attacks of xenophobic politicians, but it had grown to include six departments: Mechanical, Electrical, Civil, Agricultural, Mining, and Physics. Eighteen faculty members taught 281 students, which was almost exactly the entire size of the college in 1900. Buz Walker was the only senior faculty member to have survived the Hardy years. As we have seen, Barnes had been fired, to be replaced by Ard. Probably because he was too closely associated with Hardy to be comfortable under a new administration, Ard soon left his new post to go into the construction business in Birmingham. Of the founding faculty of the School of Engineering, only Walker remained.[27]

Hardy's departure marked the end of a period of dramatic growth. The college then entered a period of stability, which lasted until the beginning of

World War I. The School of Engineering, thus, had an opportunity to take stock of itself and try to cope with the rapid growth that had taken place under Hardy. The school also had to cope with the fact that it was desperately underfunded, understaffed, and underequipped and with the fact that it was virtually incapable of competing with other schools of engineering in the United States on anything like an equal basis.

The equipment needs of the Mechanical Engineering Department illustrated the noncompetitive situation of the School of Engineering. The equipment in the shop was essentially that which had been purchased when the shop was opened twenty years earlier. In practical terms, the only laboratory equipment available was the power plant itself. Most of the department's equipment, wrote Randle Churchill Carpenter, Ard's successor as professor of Mechanical Engineering, was out of date and would not even be legal to operate in some states because of its exposed gears and shafts. The State of Mississippi, wrote Clarence E. Reid, Head of the Electrical Engineering Department, "should not use less business judgement than a private corporation and try to use obsolete machinery simply because it will still run."[28]

These shortages were especially serious due to the fact that faculty opinion in the School of Engineering had further coalesced around the idea that shop instruction formed the basis of all technical and industrial education. As Carpenter put it, shop instruction "was essential in the training of the mechanical engineer, the electrical engineer, the civil and mining engineer, the textile engineer, the agricultural engineer, the teacher and the farmer." The requests of the faculty for new shop equipment were not extravagant— they simply wanted their students to be able to use ordinary machines customarily found in machine shops. Their equipment list included such simple items as a new grindstone, a small tool lathe, surface grinders, turret lathe, a twenty-four-inch planer, band saw, sander, jig saw, and a thirty-horsepower electric motor for operating the equipment. Providing instruction in the use of more modern technologies was also out of the question due to the lack of adequate equipment. Devices for teaching students the properties of lubricating oils, flue gasses, locomotive brakes, and automobiles were essential if students were to emerge from the college able to succeed in twentieth-century industry.[29]

Equipment for testing and evaluating the performance of steam engines was also lacking. When accurate results were required, Mechanical Engineering had to use the machinery that belonged to the power plant. Using this equipment posed a serious problem, however; only one machine existed, and if it were to "become disarranged by test," the college would be without electrical service until it could be repaired. Electrical Engineering was in a similar situation. Only one major test was ever made in the electrical engineering laboratory, wrote Professor Reid in 1913; but that test, which measured the combined output of more than one generator, was a critical one, in that it reproduced conditions found every day in the power plants of Mississippi. To perform this test and teach students other basic techniques, the department requested several small ammeters, voltmeters, and wattmeters, along with a frequency meter.[30] The only department that was satisfied in the last years of the Hardy administration was Civil Engineering, whose professor, D. W. Brown, was easy to please. In 1910, Brown informed the president that he had been able to purchase a new transit, a new level, and six drawing tables, which made his equipment adequate for his needs.[31]

Since the founding of the Mechanic Arts Department the engineering faculty had gradually assumed responsiblity for overseeing the physical plant of the institution. By the early years of this century no building was erected, plumbed, wired, or drained without the assistance of a member of the engineering faculty. The Mechanical Engineering Department maintained most of the college's equipment. Considered the most important mechanical operation on campus, the power plant had grown from an installation containing a small boiler and a forty-horsepower steam engine to a full-scale steam plant capable of producing 800 horsepower. The power plant included several smaller steam engines connected to direct current generators. The college operated two artesian wells that supplied 175 gallons of water a minute, and the Mechanical Engineering Department operated the pumping and distribution system through which water was distributed to campus consumers. The department also operated a cold storage plant and icemaking equipment. Probably because there was no better place to assign responsibility, the Mechanical Engineering Department also supervised the night-watch service and the college's fire protection system.[32]

The Electrical Engineering Department had become responsible for all the college's electrical lighting system beyond the switchboard and for directing the installation of wiring and electrical fixtures in campus buildings. As Clarence Reid noted in 1913, the duties of the members of his department were not only those of a teacher but involved those of a power plant superintendent, an electrical contractor, and often those of foreman of a wiring squad. The department head was responsible for a large amount of electrical work. In 1911, Reid and his students installed wiring in the new dormitory, the Lee Hall classrooms, the chemical laboratory, four houses, and three agricultural buildings; in addition, they rewired seven other faculty residences. "I believe that the profits on this amount of work," Reid wrote, "would have netted a contractor a very good living."[33]

The duties of the professors of mechanical and electrical engineering included overseeing the minute aspects of day-to-day management. A description of their work in 1913 illustrates how essential they had become to the college's operation. When a fuse blew in the veterinary hospital at 10:00 one night, the head of the Electrical Engineering Department left his home to get the lights back on. When a student or an employee needed a new light bulb, faculty members had to supply it. When a touring theater group came through, the faculty had to spend two days arranging lights for them. Lighting bills were made out, bids were obtained, and supplies for the campus electrical system were ordered. In short, wrote Reid, "we must be book-keepers, store-keepers, retail clerks, estimators and contractors, foremen of wiring squads composed of one or two green students; purchasing agents, and general utility men."[34] When wiring was being installed in new buildings, Reid had to be in constant attendance to oversee the unskilled student labor which was the only kind available.[35]

These duties led to power struggles between professors. In 1911, for example, Charles Ard, who had just switched departments to become the professor of mechanical engineering, wrote a long letter to President Hardy asking for control of the entire system of power production and distribution. Traditionally the Mechanical Engineering Department was responsible for generating power and sending it to the switchboard. After that, the Electrical Engineering Department took over and distributed power to campus buildings. Such a system made it difficult to assign responsibility for power failures and had led to friction between the departments. The arrangement would continue to disrupt operations in the future, wrote Ard, unless all aspects of power production and distribution were consolidated under him and the Mechanical Engineering Department.[36]

At first glance, one might think the Department of Electrical Engineering would have been happy to let Ard and his department take over some of its chores; but that was not the case. Professor Reid, for one, protested vigorously. The real issue was patronage, he said, as the two departments were the largest dispensers of nonagricultural student jobs. Reid claimed that Ard wanted to put as many student jobs as possible under his control in order to enhance his standing and that of his department. Having grown to dislike Ard, Reid rejected his suggestions on a variety of administrative grounds and accused him of unethical conduct toward the students. Reid kept notes of his conversations with Ard, citing a conversation he had with Ard in September 1909, in which Ard told him that it was his policy to seek out the leaders among the underclassmen and offer them jobs in the expectation that they would take courses in electrical engineering and that others would follow them. Students could be found, Reid went on, who had been "strongly influenced, I might say coerced, to select a certain course in order to obtain work that would permit them to remain in school." This kind of behavior, thought Reid, was a "subversion of the student labor fund." Hardy ignored their squabbles, and the situation remained unchanged.[37]

The engineering faculty were constantly complaining that their campus service work was onerous, that they needed more assistance, and, finally, that the college should make the establishment of a public service department a main priority—which, they thought, would greatly "increase the educational efficiency of both the Mechanical and Electrical Departments." Their complaints were ignored by members of the administration who held the view that campus services took precedence over everything else and were to be given a higher priority than teaching. The Electrical Engineering Department, for example, had only one suitable classroom; yet Professor Reid was compelled to use it to store "great rolls of wire." All electrical supplies were stored in campus offices and laboratories and issued from them. Working tools, such as posthole diggers, were also kept in the laboratory. Students and equipment were so crowded that they were constantly in each other's way. "I have cheerfully carried on all these matters for the past five years," wrote Clarence Reid in 1914, "although they were a great surprise to me, so totally unlike my experience in other institutions, buoyed up by the hope that at some time a part of this work would be finished."[38] Wishing to use his professional skills teaching and serving the state's electrical power industry, Reid concluded that he would never be relieved of his campus-service obligations and left the following year. He told his successor, Lucius L. Patterson, that his main reason for leaving was not the higher salary another institution had offered him but the lack of space in which to carry on his teaching duties.[39]

Normally engineering students provided much of the labor required to operate the campus services. During the early years of the century the central heating and power plants had been operated by student engineers and black firemen working under the supervision of the engineering professors and an operating engineer. In an effort to increase employment opportunities for students, Ard dismissed the black firemen and replaced them with students who, he thought, would also receive additional "educational opportunity while paying expenses." This educational opportunity could not have been gratifying. Four student firemen worked the night shift shoveling coal in shifts of three hours each. Students also operated the night-watch service and served as heating and plumbing attendants in the dormitories and other campus buildings. Electrical Engineering students performed most of the work involving the distribution of electricity.[40]

Inevitably the extensive reliance on student labor for maintaining campus services led to problems stemming from student indifference, inattention, and ignorance. Student crews botched the wiring of Lee Hall, for example, apparently forgetting to install a main switch so that the lights in the first floor hall could not be turned off during the day. The hall had been plastered and the fixtures installed before the mistake was discovered.[41] The slowness of the state in providing new equipment was especially serious on campus because machines deteriorated more quickly when maintained by students. In a factory, wrote Professor Carpenter, machines could be expected to last eight to ten years when expert workmen were using them. Campus machines, while not used as constantly, actually received rougher service because the students were generally "absolutely unfamiliar with caring for and handling machines of any kind." Carpenter's colleague, Reid, was forced to wire buildings with no assistance other than a few preparatory students who had never handled a wire before.[42]

The boll weevil had arrived in full force during the early years of the century, and Mississippi agriculture was in a depressed condition. Consequently, faculty salaries were low and the School of Engineering had great difficulty retaining qualified staff members. Faculty were constantly leaving for more remunerative positions. When that happened they often were replaced by recent recipients of bachelor's degrees from Mississippi A & M. The idea that the college could "break in" new men quickly was a fallacy, thought Robert Gay, professor of Civil Engineering. In larger schools where there were several instructors in a department, Gay wrote, the inexperience of one or two new instructors could do less harm than at Mississippi A & M where the new man was almost always the only instructor. Even during poor economic times it was not always possible to find new graduates to accept these posts. In 1914, a desperate Electrical Engineering Department was unsuccessfully trying to find an assistant. Reid and Walker had canvassed all the graduates of the classes of 1910 to 1913, trying to find "anyone suitable who could be induced to return." Finally, in desperation they employed a member of the senior class to teach other undergraduates.43

Due to the low salaries and abusive administrative policies it had become all but impossible to employ a stable teaching faculty. "Some definite policy must be adopted," wrote Gay, "which will place us on an equality with other schools so that we can obtain good men and keep them more than one year." He urged the president to find a way to promise new faculty members a raise for their second year, which he thought would be an incentive to keep them on the staff. Gay also recommended changing a pernicious administrative policy which involved paying faculty members the same salaries ordinarily given to men employed for nine months but requiring them to remain in attendance for the entire year unless they were given special permission to leave by the president. Lucius Patterson, for example, taught at Mississippi A & M for seven years before he was authorized to take a summer vacation. This meant that, unlike professors at most other colleges and universities, faculty members were not free to increase their earnings during the summer.44

Teaching loads for the faculty were extremely high and would probably have soon driven today's faculty members into other professions. For example, Professor Ard was scheduled to spend thirty-four hours per week in the classroom besides performing other duties associated with the campus electrical service. The department's associate professor taught thirty-five hours per week, and its instructor taught thirty hours. In 1911, a recent graduate who had joined the Electrical Engineering and Physics faculty taught thirty-seven hours per week, spent the rest of his daylight hours supervising the student wiring crew, and used his evenings to grade exercises and prepare lessons. As Patterson dryly pointed out, this left "but little time for recreation and broadening reading."45

The engineering building erected with such enthusiasm in 1904 by

Professors Ard and Barnes was suffering from the college's efforts to operate on a shoestring. It was falling apart, largely due to attempts to skimp on construction costs. The building was no longer suitable for the needs of the engineering departments. Dust, plaster, mortar, and other grit constantly sifted through the upper floor, contaminating the equipment housed below. Also, the floors were not strong enough to prevent vibrations from heavy equipment from spreading throughout the building, which damaged instruments and prevented accurate measurement.[46]

A variety of factors contributed to the desperate condition of the college and its School of Engineering. Appropriations were constantly meager, in part because Mississippi's cotton-based economy was suffering greatly from the ravages of the boll weevil, and in part because Mississippi's governors and lesser politicians had little interest in higher education in general and technical education in particular. President Hardy's policy of encouraging growth regardless of available resources was also to blame. The entrance examination had disappeared. Any white student who had graduated from an accredited high school was welcome to attend Mississippi A & M. The size of the faculty and the number of classrooms and offices never caught up to the growth in student population. "Our school would do the state a much greater service," wrote Robert Gay, "and would have a much better reputation at home and abroad, if our attendance were to be cut down one third or one half by raising the entrance requirements and the standard of scholarship." During this period higher education was becoming more politicized than ever.[47]

Hardy's successors, George R. Hightower and William Hall Smith, owed their appointments to support from newly elected governors. With such uncertain tenure they were unwilling to accompany their ideas for new programs with vigorous requests for increased funds. Hightower's most important legacy was the establishment of a program in business. This program was needed, he thought, because most merchants were antagonistic to farmers and were often interested mainly in exploiting tenant farmers. Therefore, it was important to train future merchants to think along lines friendly to the farmer. On the other hand, farmers must learn to protect themselves from merchants and must learn to meet the merchant on his own ground.

These were interesting and persuasive arguments; a program in business was certainly appropriate for an institution charged with educating the industrial classes. The problem arose when Hightower insisted that the program could be started with no new money. In his biennial report to the legislature he stated: *"It is very largely nothing but a problem of recombining what we already have to provide for the wants of this class of students."* [48]

The attitude that more could always be done with less was especially harmful to the School of Engineering, with its need for laboratory equipment and supplies. Mississippi A & M had simply become incapable of offering a program in engineering comparable to that available in other states. The institution was imposing a handicap on Mississippi boys, thought Gay, by sending them into the engineering field with less training than they could get in similar institutions in almost any other state in the Union.[49]

Gay realized that the funding situation was so bad that disaster was imminent. He had learned that the Carnegie Foundation was planning to undertake a study of engineering schools in the United States that would be a companion to its devastating study of American medical education published in 1910. Foreseeing an almost unending struggle with accreditation agencies, Gay warned President Hightower that a national survey would not be a pleasant experience. "I only need call your attention to the effects of the inspection of the schools of medicine," he told Hightower, "to impress you with the fact that it will be little glory for us to be found at the bottom of the list of Engineering Schools, and frankly, I know of no other engineering school of collegiate pretensions which maintains so low a standard as our own."[50]

Clearly the School of Engineering was on the edge of a precipice. By the outbreak of World War I it had a core of dedicated faculty members, the beginning of an equipment collection, and a curriculum that was beginning to approximate that of older and better institutions. The wealth of the state would soon increase, President Smith predicted in his first official speech, and the people of Mississippi would see fit to double the plant of Mississippi A & M.[51] His optimism was undoubtedly appreciated by the faculty of the School of Engineering, who desperately needed additional resources. Unfortunately, Smith's optimism was unfounded—Mississippi A & M and its School of Engineering were about to enter the most trying decades in the institution's history.

Chapter Three

The Struggle for Survival

On April 6, 1917 the United States entered World War I initiating a period of turmoil and change that transformed most American institutions. Mississippi A & M College and its School of Engineering were not immune from this influence. The effect of the war on the School of Engineering could not be predicted, Buz Walker told President William Hall Smith, who had succeeded George Hightower in 1916, adding that he hoped he would soon receive instructions from Washington regarding the role the Engineering School might be expected to play in the war. He did not have to wait long. Students who were already advanced members of the Reserve Officers Training Corps left for service almost immediately, and many others returned to the farms in order to contribute to the war effort by helping to produce food. So thoroughgoing was the disruption that classes were dismissed on May 18, 1917 instead of May 28 and commencement for that year was cancelled. For the next two years regular instruction was more or less abandoned due to the demands made on the school to provide specialized technical training for servicemen and because the few regular students who remained were in such a state of uncertainty that they could not put forth their best efforts.[1]

Faculty members, too, were soon affected by the war. Financially squeezed between salaries that had not risen appreciably since the turn of the century and increases in the cost of living that accompanied the outbreak of war, they saw their standard of living decline. The effect on the School of Engineering was out of proportion to the rest of the college because men with engineering skills were so much in demand. As long as young men could get $2,000 to $2,500 per year in the army, wrote Professor T. G. Gladney of Civil Engineering, and from $3.00 to $6.00 per day in industry, "we will get nothing but the weaklings in our work."[2]

The departments of the Engineering School quickly found themselves heavily involved in providing war-training programs. Overall, some 3,000 men attended Mississippi A & M College as part of the War Department's Student Army Training Corps (SATC) program. The Physics Department used its expertise to provide instruction in the new technology of radio. Federal funds allowed construction of a small transmitter which the department used to provide training to several hundred students. The departments of geology and civil engineering provided special instruction to SATC students in surveying, map preparation, and mapreading. This type of instruction which required the departments to completely alter their methods of instruction was made particularly difficult because equipment had become scarce due to the demands of the war. Fortunately the College possessed a well-equipped wood shop capable of manufacturing the drawing tables that were unavailable in the marketplace.[3]

The department that benefitted the most from World War I was Agricultural Engineering. It was immediately transformed from a nondescript part of the School of Agriculture to a full-fledged member of the School of Engineering. The war had caused severe manpower shortages in Mississippi which, coupled with calls for increased production of food and fiber, led to a high demand for the department's services. The department held a series of "tractor schools" that were attended by several thousand farmers as well as a variety of short courses for farmers both at Mississippi A & M and in other towns around the state. The high prices Mississippi farmers received for cotton during the war resulted in a rural building boom. Agricultural Engineers responded by sending farmers blueprints and instructions for building barns, silos and even residences. The department even used its expertise to reach a much different constituency—the urban housewife. Labor shortages during war had created a scarcity of washer women, and the department's Farm Engineering specialist worked with the Home Economics Department to promote the use of washing machines. Eventually Mississippi housewives purchased a thousand machines.[4]

Another part of Agricultural Engineering's contribution to the war effort was training soldiers to use motorized vehicles. Between 600 and 700 men who were part of the motor transport service received training in operating and repairing trucks and cars. The department also established a garage which did commercial repair work on automobiles, tractors, and other farm machinery powered by gasoline engines. Maintained for several years after the war as a money-making operation, the garage soon became part of the campus service system. The college, of course, had long relied heavily on its ability to combine the technological expertise of the engineering faculty with cheap student labor to serve the campus, and the garage was an extension of this philosophy. Buz Walker soon discovered, however, that using student labor to operate a campus service such as the power plant, where money was transferred through established accounts, was much different from using it to operate a commercial operation, where small amounts of cash were constantly changing hands. After incurring serious losses the garage was discontinued in 1921 as "unsatisfactory and undesirable."[5]

Perhaps the most important reflection of the new status of the Agricultural Engineering Department was the establishment of a degree program in Agricultural Engineering within the School of Engineering. Throughout the history of Mississippi A & M Agricultural Engineering had occupied a somewhat confused administrative position. Having begun life in 1878 as the Department of Rural Engineering, it was one of the school's oldest departments. A Department of Civil and Rural Engineering emerged in 1901, and Civil and Rural Engineering became part of the School of Engineering when it came into existence in 1902. In 1903, however, the department moved back to the School of Agriculture, while Civil Engineering, after absorbing Drawing, remained part of the School of Engineering. Rural Engineering was renamed Agricultural Engineering in 1910, although it remained in the School of Agriculture.[6]

During the War the Federal Government made great efforts to stimulate the production of food. Congress appropriated large sums for agricultural colleges to use in helping expand production. Mississippi A & M received $145,000 for this purpose during the fiscal year 1919 which almost doubled the amount other state and federal sources had provided. A large portion of these funds were used to increase the level of mechanization in Mississippi agriculture. During the war county agents—who at least in regard to mechanization, were supervised by the Agricultural Engineering Department—persuaded Mississippi farmers to buy 31,000 new farm implements. Under these circumstances the demand for trained agricultural engineers became acute; the School of Engineering decided to take advantage of the situation by establishing a four-year course leading to a bachelor of science degree in agricultural engineering. The School of Engineering took special pains to distinguish its program from the traditional "nontechnical" program in the School of Agriculture. The program was specifically designed to train engineers to cope with the engineering problems pertaining to agricultural equipment and to "master soil, drainage, and building problems with precision and yet not get so far away from the farmer that his work is lost."[7]

Before the war agricultural engineering possessed a highly practical curriculum designed for students who wished to work in medium-and large-scale agriculture. Students took courses in such subjects as Farm Machinery, Farm Buildings, and Concrete Construction. Seniors were allowed an elective course in Spraying Apparatus, while two courses in farm mechanics provided them with training in harnessing horses, operating farm machinery, tying and splicing ropes, and lacing belts. The only mathematics required involved the kinds of arithmetic and trigonometry needed to survey and measure land and to lay out buildings.[8]

The establishment in 1919 of a degree program in the School of Engineering bifurcated the department. The department retained its practical courses for agricultural students while instituting a new degree, which E. R. Gross, the new department head, proudly claimed would be "on a par with the Mechanical, Electrical, Civil and Architectural Engineering degrees."[9]

The end of World War I did not end Mississippi A & M's institutional turmoil. Even though entrance requirements had been raised, students returned in record-breaking numbers. Certainly the composition of the student body was much different. The usual crop of teenage boys was joined by veterans who wanted to get on with their lives which had been interrupted by the war. These men were joined by others sent by the Federal Board of Vocational Education (established to prepare disabled veterans for the skilled trades). As a result of this program three new groups of men emerged. The first group included students who were capable of pursuing ordinary college courses leading to a regular college degree; the second group was composed of men unprepared for college, but who could profit by college-level instruction; and the third group consisted of illiterates who required a program in elementary education before they could benefit from technical instruction. The last group was completely unprepared for the instruction offered, but these students made up a sizable component of the student body; during the 1921-22 session they comprised 449 of 1593 students. Their presence must have had a depressing effect on the tone of the college and the faculty did not quite know how to deal with them. The college recommended that the Vocational Education board find another place for them and the program ended in August, 1921.[10]

The war had placed great strain on campus facilities, and the campus was far from ready to receive the number of students who appeared in 1919; classroom space, dormitory rooms, and trained faculty members were woefully inadequate. Three or four students occupied two-man rooms in the dormitories. New staff members could not always find accommodations either on campus or in Starkville, and several had to send their families away. Campus services had suffered greatly as a result of the war. The power plant was hard hit by the great increase in the cost of fuel and labor resulting from the war and from the fluctuations in the number of regular students and special trainees. The general decline in the number of students had lowered income, but the cost of providing heat, water and light had remained practically the same. Collecting utility bills from the trainees attending school for a few months at a time had been nearly impossible. When Randle Churchill Carpenter took over the management of the power plant in September 1918, he found its accounts to be seriously in arrears. Indeed, the stresses placed on the institution during World War I had made it very difficult to carry on the College's commercial activities in a businesslike fashion, and the debts incurred by the power plant, the automobile garage and other services eventually led to a serious financial scandal. In 1920, auditors found that the College was short $140,000, a situation which, coupled with political difficulties, forced President Smith to resign.[11]

Although the rhythm of education had been disrupted by the war, several of the engineering departments prospered during the war years. For the first time faculty members who had never been part of the extension service felt the benefit of direct funding from federal sources. State appropriations had sunk so low that the engineering departments could not afford to pay for equipment to be repaired. Had it not been for federal aid, wrote Professor

Lucious L. Patterson, Electrical Engineering could not have carried on its work. The Physics Department was particularly proud of the radio station it had installed using federal money.[12]

The war brought with it dramatically increased prices for cotton and foodstuffs and thus created an economic boom in Mississippi that was unprecedented in the state's post-Civil War history. Although this prosperity disappeared with the end of the war, it did create a temporary willingness on the part of the legislature to provide increased funding for state services. In 1919, the legislature approved the issuing of bonds to be used for the improvement of state institutions. It also approved a construction program that specifically authorized Mississippi A & M to build a new library. The engineering faculty did not seem very enthusiastic about the prospect of a new library building. The library had always maintained a low position on the School of Engineering's list of priorities. In 1925, for example, the school requested $6,000 for machine shop equipment, $5,000 for wood shop equipment, and $100 for books and magazines. The Engineering faculty was very dissatisfied with its quarters in the old Engineering building; because "engineers seldom visit[ed] the general library" the Engineering faculty supported efforts to improve the Engineering buildings instead of investing money in a new library building.[13]

Although blueprints and specifications had been drawn up for a new library, the State Bond Improvement Commission which was responsible for spending the bond money failed to carry out the intent of the legislature and eliminated the library from the list of improvements to be made at Mississippi A & M. Instead of a new library the college got a new power plant and a science building (now Harned Hall), where the top floor was reserved for the library. The commission also authorized a renovation of the Engineering Building so extensive as to make it virtually a new building.[14]

Thus, the School of Engineering became one of the main beneficiaries of the bond program. The old Engineering building, built in 1905, was inadequate almost from the day it was occupied. The power plant filled the east wing of the building, the north wing contained the forge, and the south wing housed the wood shop. The three-story main building contained all the offices, laboratories and classrooms.[15] The poor construction of the main building and its wings caused them to deteriorate quickly. Professors Barnes and Ard, who had served as construction superintendents, were proud of their ability to erect the building for much less than commercial bidders; but it soon became clear that theirs' had been false economies. Saving money had resulted in a weak and inadequate building. The foundations of the first Engineering building still exist in the basement of McCain Hall, which was built over much of the old building. Inspection of this foundation makes clear one reason for the rapid demise of the first building: Ard and Barnes had used soft and porous brick for the building's foundations which was unable to withstand the vibrations caused by the heavy machinery in the laboratories.

The result of the Bond Commission's work was a renovation of the Engineering Building so extensive that the School of Engineering possessed an almost new building that, for the first time provided adequate space for classrooms and laboratories plus space in which to install a steam and gas laboratory. The drawing and geology rooms and offices were installed on the third floor of the new building, along with the telephone laboratory. Civil Engineering and Physics occupied the second floor. Electrical Engineering was located in the south wing near the dean's office and the north wing contained the shops, forge, and foundry. The Engineering Library and the Mechanical Engineering office were located in the two main rooms near the building's entrance.[16] Because funds ran out before the building could be furnished, the departments had to use their own meager resources for such things as special doors, desks, lecture tables, and storage facilities.[17]

The School of Engineering was indeed fortunate to be able to have taken advantage of the wartime prosperity. The fortunes of the State of Mississippi declined dramatically after the war. It is part of the lore of U.S. history that the stock market crash of 1929 ended the prosperity of the "Roaring 20s" and began the economic depression that lasted almost until the outbreak of World War II. While this may have been true for certain parts of the United States, most rural states whose economies were based on agriculture suffered from depressed conditions almost from the end of World War I until the beginning of World War II. Mississippi was especially hard hit. In spite of the heroic efforts of the Cooperative Extension Service to encourage farmers to diversify, the state's economy remained based on the price of cotton, which remained low throughout the 1920s and 30s.

Buz Walker, acutely aware of the economic hardship that accompanied the state's dependence on a one-crop economy, took every opportunity to remind others of the perils inherent in the state's obsession with cotton and its unwillingness to encourage industrialization. "The engineer has an important mission," he wrote,

> even in a State devoted so largely to agriculture. It must be plain that industrial and economic independence can not be based safely on agriculture alone. Industrial progress based upon engineering must accompany agricultural development. Enduring and far-reaching prosperity and national independence will require the united efforts of agriculture and industry, and the engineer is destined to take an increasingly important share in the future development of our State as well as of the nation. A country with great natural resources and with men trained in all lines of agriculture and in every division of engineering may turn its face to the future with a confidence that is born of prosperity and grows with the consciousness of power.[18]

Variations on this comment appeared in official documents of the college throughout the 1920s. Walker's observations carried little weight with the state legislature, however, and appropriations declined dramatically. The college eliminated programs, dismissed staff members, and put off replacing aged equipment. The decade of the 1920s was largely marked by retrenchment and unending efforts to maintain the levels of quality that had been achieved before the War.

The first casualties of the postwar depression were the new programs that the School of Engineering had instituted in the flush of wartime prosperity. In 1920, a four-year program in architectural engineering was grafted on to the drawing department, which itself had been separated from civil engineering in 1918. Although the engineering faculty generally assumed that architecture was a fine art, they had established the department so that students would be taught to understand the practical and technical requirements closely connecting architecture to the other branches of engineering. Most of the courses in the curriculum already existed in other departments. Students took Masonry Building Construction and Concrete Design from the civil engineers, Electrical Illumination and Wiring for Light and Power from electrical engineers, and Mechanics and Mechanics of Materials from mechanical engineers. The courses unique to the architectural engineering curriculum were History of Architecture, Charcoal Drawing, Pen and Ink Rendering, Water Color Painting, History of Art, and Antique Drawing. These courses were taught by the department head, Matthew Freeman, an accomplished artist and probably the instigator of the program. For the first time fine arts had become part of the Mississippi A & M College curriculum.[19]

Although student demand for Architectural Engineering was fairly high and was comparable to that existing in several of the more established departments, abolishing it saved the salary of one faculty member. Freeman protested vigorously and a group of students circulated a petition urging the program's reinstatement. Walker rejected all pro-architecture arguments, however. Students interested in this line of work, he thought, could take degrees in civil engineering and then pursue postgraduate studies in another institution where architectural engineering was stressed. The School eliminated Architectural Engineering in 1922.[20]

Agricultural Engineering, which had benefited the most from the war, was the department that suffered the most from the postwar budget cuts. Its entry into the School of Engineering was abruptly terminated, and once again it found itself solely a School of Agriculture department. As a result of decreased appropriations, E. R. Gross who had been instrumental in instituting the engineering degree program in Agricultural Engineering left the college in 1922, and the program in the School of Engineering disappeared with him. Of the twenty staff members forced to leave when the budget was reduced, four were from agricultural engineering.[21]

The budget cuts, combined with the pitifully low existing salary levels, demoralized the faculty. Instructors' salaries, for example, were reduced from $500 to $425 and assistants found their salaries reduced to $1,500 per year. Hiring assistant professors at these salaries, wrote Gladney, was all but impossible, especially considering the enormous teaching loads they were expected to carry. Members of the faculty were constantly begging for salary increases in their reports during the postwar years. Matthew Freeman, the venerable head of drawing, for example, had taught at Mississippi A & M for twenty years; yet he still did not receive the maximum salary paid to other department heads, nor did he have the use of a campus house. "Most of the satisfaction of being in the profession [of college teaching]," he wrote, "comes from knowing that you are helping humanity to a higher plane; still, that knowledge will not supply the comforts, nay, not even the necessities of old age." Howard W. Moody, who succeeded Walker as dean of the School of Engineering, expressed similar sentiments in 1927. A dean worthy of his position, he wrote, "has continually at heart the interests of the School; he is studying every matter which may lead to raising standards, bettering its good name and reputation, and, by the outsiders, has placed upon him much blame for any failure or shortcomings." A salary of $4,500, he thought, would be sufficient "to distinguish and dignify the office." The net effect of the desperate financial situation was to drive away every member of the School of Engineering faculty not from Mississippi and nearly all those possessing advanced degrees.[22]

Clearly, those who chose to stay at Mississippi A & M were there because of their Mississippi roots. A list of the sixteen members of the engineering faculty remaining in 1924 shows that nearly all were from small Mississippi towns. Only Walker and Moody possessed the Ph.D. degree, and their degrees were in mathematics and physics. Only three—Gladney, Patterson, and Moody—had earned master's degrees. The rest had B.S. degrees or, as was the case with two instructors, had no degree at all. Nearly all of the faculty had been students at Mississippi A & M.[23]

In spite of the depressed state of the School of Engineering, students who saw an engineering degree as a way out of the grinding poverty that surrounded agriculture continued to choose the program. By 1925, nearly as many students were enrolled in the School of Engineering as were in the School of Agriculture. Enrollments continued to increase until, by 1927, engineering surpassed agriculture as the largest school of the college. That year the school presented the largest list of seniors eligible for graduation.[24]

Considerable overcrowding resulted as a result of insufficient space and equipment. A basic civil engineering course was taught to forty-two students in a classroom that had thirty-two seats. Five or six seniors in civil engineering had to share space at one drawing board, and they had no lockers or cabinets in which to store their equipment. Little new equipment could be purchased both because of a general decline in appropriations, and because the departments were forced to use the funds available for equipment to purchase furniture for classrooms, laboratories, and offices in the new engineering building. Thus, most of the equipment that arrived on campus resulted from gifts and loans by manufacturers. In 1925, Patterson attended a trade conference on electrical products and returned very pleased with himself because he had managed to persuade the Southern Bell and Cumberland telephone companies to donate equipment to set up an artificial line that simulated the problems involved in the long-distance transmission of speech. Electrical Engineering received several gifts from the General Electric Company. While obtaining equipment in this way did not require an outlay of cash, it did tend to put the engineering departments at the mercy of the manufacturers.[25]

Buz Walker became President of Mississippi A & M in July 1925, succeeding David Carlisle Hull, who had served from 1920 to 1925. Walker was the most distinguished scholar that had ever been associated with the School of Engineering, even though his advanced degrees were in mathematics, not engineering. He had achieved some fame in the world of mathematics by being the first to solve a complex mathematical problem of long standing. Walker was also one of the few members of the Mississippi A & M faculty who had spent much time in more prestigious institutions of higher learning. Within the constraints imposed by the objective conditions at Mississippi A & M, he did what he could to place the institution in the ranks of nationally recognized colleges and universities.[26]

Walker's first step in this direction was to gain accreditation for the college. Until 1926, the only recognition that hinted at accreditation was a decision in 1913 by the Civil Service Bureau, in the Engineering Division of the War Department, to place Mississippi A & M on its list of "Approved Technical Schools." The bureau's action was meaningless in the academic world, however, and the institution's failure to meet regional and national standards made it difficult for students to transfer credits earned at Mississippi A & M to other institutions or to have their degrees recognized in other states. Even Louisiana, a state not known for its commitment to excellence in education in the 1920s, refused to place Mississippi A & M on the list of institutions approved by its State Board of Engineering Examiners. Walker was determined to remedy this situation.[27]

The first and most important step was to gain recognition by the Association of Colleges and Secondary Schools of the Southern States (now the Southern Association of Colleges and Schools). Walker approached the association with an inquiry about the standards Mississippi A & M would be required to meet. In 1926, after instituting a series of reforms that upgraded admission requirements and the quality of general education, Walker applied for membership, and the college was accepted that fall. Accreditation meant that Mississippi A & M was also eligible to join the American Council on Education.[28]

Walker was especially interested in seeing the School of Engineering gain as much national recognition as it could. He used the 1926 accreditation to gain recognition by national engineering associations. One of the ways colleges and universities measure their quality is through the establishment of chapters of national honorary societies. Walker understood this fact of academic life and used the college's newly-won recognition by the Southern Association to support applications for a chapter of Tau Beta Pi, the national engineering honorary society, and for a student chapter of the American Society of Mechanical Engineers. In his search for national recognition Walker used the rather dubious arguments that the institution's recognition by the Civil Service Bureau meant that it was "recognized and placed on equality with leading schools of the country," and that its membership in the Association of Colleges and Secondary Schools meant that it was rated as an "A-1 college." Nevertheless, he succeeded, and an ASME chapter was started in September 1926 followed by Tau Beta Pi in December 1928. Walker was pleased with his work. By 1930, thirty departments were housed in five distinct schools, and 150 faculty and staff members were employed in the academic divisions serving over 1,500 students. Indeed, wrote Walker, these were "crowning years."[29]

All hopes that Mississippi A & M would take its place alongside the major colleges and universities of the United States were dashed in 1930 though the massive interference of state politics in the internal operations of the state's educational institutions. The modern-day recognition, by nearly all institutions of higher learning, of the importance of faculty tenure and academic freedom in insulating higher education from factional politics makes it difficult to appreciate the role that electoral politics has played in higher education in Mississippi throughout much of its history. Traditionally, governors of the state appointed all members of the various institutional governing boards. These appointees were chosen because of their willingness to follow the governor's political agenda. In large part this system was due to the prevailing attitude toward gubernatorial power in state government. A long-standing presumption held that governors headed the state's educational system in the same way that they headed the state militia. Governor Vardaman, for example, had stacked the board of trustees of the University of Mississippi in 1906 to obtain the dismissal of Chancellor Robert Fulton. As noted previously, President Hardy knew better than to try to remain President of Mississippi A & M after the election of Governor Brewer. Governor Theodore G. Bilbo bragged during his first election campaign that he planned to "kick out" President Hightower with a "special pair of boots"—and in 1916, Bilbo did just that. Four years later, Governor Lee Russell used the pretext of wartime finanical arrears to oust Hightower's successor, W. H. Smith.30

Although the appointments of presidents Hull and Walker were relatively free of political interference, there was no assurance that it had disappeared. In 1928 Bilbo returned to the governor's mansion for a second term with a pledge to transform Mississippi's institutions of higher education. His predecessor, Henry Whitfield, had commissioned Michael V. O'Shea of the University of Wisconsin to prepare a full-scale study of Mississippi's educational system in 1927. O'Shea had recommended a series of dramatic and sweeping changes that, if implemented, would have created a unified system of higher education in Mississippi similar to the one that existed in the State of Wisconsin. In his second inaugural address Bilbo promised to implement O'Shea's proposed reforms by moving the University of Mississippi to Jackson and turning the Oxford campus into a teacher's college.31

Unlike many of his predecessors, Bilbo did not have complete control of Mississippi's institutions of higher education. Mainly as a result of the battle between Governor Vardaman and Chancellor Fulton, the legislature had changed the system of governance prevailing in Mississippi's institutions of higher learning. In 1910 the legislature had placed the University of Mississippi, Mississippi A & M College, Alcorn A & M, and the Industrial Institute and College (now Mississippi University for Women) under one governing board. This board was not as easy to manage as the independent boards had been, and Bilbo was at first unable to implement his ideas. Opposition to his reform plans came from all quarters—the state's educational institutions opposed him at every turn and both the legislature and the board refused to implement his schemes. By 1930, Bilbo had decided to transform higher education in Mississippi by executive action. He had finally gained control of the board of trustees through additional appointments and prepared to change the institutions by replacing those leaders and faculty members who disagreed with him.32

He struck in the summer of 1930. At its meeting on July 13, the board of trustees fired hundreds of administrators and faculty members throughout the state, including Buz Walker and Howard Moody. Bilbo's board replaced Walker with Hugh Critz, an academic gadfly who possessed no advanced degree. He had previously held several positions at Mississippi A & M and before 1930 was employed by the public relations department of Mississippi Power and Light. Mississippi A & M was the hardest hit; between twenty and twenty-five faculty members, out of a total of ninety-one, lost their positions, and around one hundred agricultural extension and college support staff were fired. Although Bilbo asserted that he was only trying to implement the recommendations of the O'Shea report, he showed his contempt for higher education through his dismissals by targeting those with advanced degrees. In the School of Engineering, for example, Walker and Moody were the only two with Ph.D. degrees and both were sacked. The third engineering faculty member fired was Thomas Gladney, one of the few possessing a master's degree. "How unfortunate, tragically unfortunate," wrote Walker, "was the meeting of the Board of Trustees . . . which stands without parallel in the educational history of the American Government."[33]

The effect of Bilbo's actions on the School of Engineering and on Mississippi A & M were immediate and devastating. The Southern Association of Colleges and Secondary Schools immediately launched an investigation of Mississippi higher education and in December 1930 voted to suspend Mississippi A & M, the University of Mississippi, the State Teachers College (now the University of Southern Mississippi), and the renamed Mississippi State College for Women from membership effective September 1, 1931. National academic associations also removed Mississippi A & M and the state's other colleges and universities from their lists of approved institutions. The American Association of Colleges and Universities, the American Medical Association, the American Association of Law Schools, the American Association of University Women, the American Chemical Society, and the American Association of University Professors all censured Bilbo's actions and dropped Mississippi's institutions of higher learning from their lists of approved colleges and universities.[34]

The School of Engineering, like the rest of the institution, experienced a major loss of credibility. In the fall of 1930, the American Society of Civil Engineers dropped Mississippi A & M and the University of Mississippi from membership, noting that "the summary dismissal of so large a number of the faculties of the two schools [does] not make for suitable instruction in engineering." In addition, the statement went on, the student chapters of the society at the two schools would be discontinued. Governor Bilbo responded by announcing that if the A.S.C.E did not approve of his July firings "then no one should care whether they belong to the association or not."35

Lucious L. Patterson, who had succeeded Moody as dean of the School of Engineering, quickly embarked on a course designed to control the damage casued by Bilbo's actions. Realizing that withdrawal of accreditation would have a serious impact on the confidence of students and parents in Mississippi A & M, he wrote to several firms that had employed School of Engineering graduates in the past, asking them to comment on the effect the removal of accreditation from Mississippi A & M might have. Patterson reported that the response from the firms was positive and that the withdrawal of accreditation would cause little change in their employment policies, although the anonymous author of the single response that Dean Patterson quoted in his press release was in truth extremely cautious in his willingness to continue employing Mississippi A & M graduates. In fact, removal of accreditation from the college did make it difficult for engineering graduates to find employment, and they suffered along with their professors. Fearing that credits earned at Mississippi A & M would not be recognized by employers, many students transferred to out-of-state institutions. Whereas, before 1931, graduates generally had little difficulty finding entry-level positions as engineers, many post-deaccreditation graduates found that they could be promoted to that grade only after a probationary period as a laborer.36

Bilbo and his board of trustees soon tried unsuccessfully to persuade the various academic associations, particularly the Southern Association, to retract their censures. Mississippi A & M and its sister institutions remained on the blacklist until 1932, when Bilbo's successor, Martin S. Conner, tried to remove higher education from politics by establishing a new board of trustees. This one was charged with overseeing all state institutions of higher learning. Its members served staggered twelve-year terms which was supposed to prevent any single governor from gaining control of it. Declaring itself to be devoted to "sound business and proper ethical principles free from political or partisan considerations," the new board persuaded the Southern Association to provisionally reinstate the state's institutions, and they were awarded full membership in 1934.37

Although by 1934, most outside professional agencies had restored Mississippi A & M to their lists of approved institutions, the college now found itself faced with an even more serious threat: the economic depression that gripped the United States throughout the 1930s. Traditionally, the Mississippi legislature had met on a biennial basis and made appropriations for two years at a time. By 1931, revenues coming into the state treasury were barely half of what had been appropriated for the year. The result was total financial chaos, which resulted in unpaid salaries, freezes on the purchase of equipment and supplies, and near-elimination of routine maintenance on campus buildings. The engineering departments were especially hard-hit by the budget cuts, due to the fact that they were so dependent on their equipment for instruction and because engineering students routinely used up large quantities of materials in their work: The Department of Electrical Engineering, for example, had been given an appropriation of $3000 for the 1930-32 biennium but had been permitted to spend only $500 of it. When Professor Patterson prepared an emergency revised budget for the period July 1, 1932-December 1, 1933, he eliminated all expenditures for equipment and repairs in the Department of Electrical Engineering and decreased the same budget category for the power plant by two-thirds. All other categories except student labor, which was halved, were decreased by an average of 32 percent. In order to teach students to test the strength of reinforced concrete, the Civil Engineering Department was forced to solicit donations of equipment and supplies. Moreover, the department had been instructed to use such new funds as came available to make up the deficits in the payroll. Stocks of consumable materials in every department fell to practically nothing.[38]

Both faculty and students quickly found their lives thrown into turmoil. Although Mississippi A & M engineering students had been forced to cope with many problems stemming from inadequate facilities over the years, finding positions after graduation had rarely been one of them. The Depression changed the situation, and few graduates in the class of 1931 were able to obtain employment after graduation. The Engineering faculty was hit hard by the economic crisis. In 1932, the legislature had decreased appropriations to the college by 42 percent which resulted in numerous layoffs and an overall salary reduction of 25 percent. Those not laid off must have appreciated what salaries they did get since they had not been paid at all during the first half of 1932. They seemed to accept their situation stoically and continued to teach their classes. The much-abused Freeman dryly told President Hugh Critz that thirty hours of teaching per week would leave few daylight hours for grading drawings but then loyally promised not to complain if the future held even heavier teaching loads and smaller salaries. The Civil Engineering Department, wrote Dewey McCain in 1933, was constantly being asked to perform tests on brick, concrete, and other building materials by state contractors, even though no money had been appropriated for such work. As McCain told Dean Patterson, "We have always submitted bills for such services and have just as regularly failed to collect, and we have never insisted."39

Critz, who had gained his position as a result of the Bilbo episode, seemed confused by the enormity of the political, academic, and financial blows the institution was absorbing. In an odd report on the biennium he began by painting a rosy situation at the college, noting that "Mississippi State College has just completed a splendid academic session, one of the best I have ever actually known." He then reversed himself and informed his readers that the college had been laboring under great strain because it followed instructions to "cut off the dog's tail at one fell swoop." Necessary supplies had not been purchased, and many employees had been forced to take unpaid leaves of absence. "You must not expect," he continued, "for us to continue to compete with and win from the best and strongest financially equipped institutions in the land." As things stood the college was in danger of becoming the laughing stock of the Association of Land Grant Colleges.40

Although Bilbo and the Depression had provided enough misery for one decade, a third event soon assaulted the college's ability to serve the students of the state. In 1932, the new board of trustees decided to explore the feasibility of developing a unitary system of higher education in Mississippi. As mentioned above, the traditional system of governance had allowed each institution to develop independently of the others. Each institution had its own board of trustees and the legislature usually approved the recommendations of the boards. In 1932, a section of the law creating the board of trustees required that each institution be assigned a role in what was supposed to be a coordinated system of higher education. Uncertain as to how go about this herculean task, the board commissioned a study by the Division of Surveys and Field Studies at George Peabody College to advise them on creating a coordinated system of higher education in Mississippi.41

The Peabody Report, or "The Survey," as it was called on campus, recommended sweeping changes in both the University of Mississippi and

Mississippi A & M College (renamed Mississippi State College in 1932). In essence the report recommended purifying the two institutions by removing all technical and engineering curricula from the University of Mississippi and by abolishing the schools of science and business at Mississippi State College. Mississippi State, it argued, should confine itself to "practical and technological problems," while the University of Mississippi should concentrate on the liberal arts and professional training. It further recommended that the senior colleges remodel themselves so as to be mainly providers of upper-division work, leaving basic lower-division instruction to the state's junior colleges.[42]

Clearly, adoption of the report's findings would have been devastating to Mississippi State College. If strictly implemented the Peabody Report would have transformed Mississippi State College into a small vocational-technical institution offering only upper-division instruction in agriculture and engineering. Though rid of competition from the University of Mississippi, the School of Engineering would have been severely weakened. Elimination of the School of Science would have taken away an important element of engineering education, which, by the 1930s, was becoming more scientific and less shop-oriented. Establishing a strict lower- and upper-division system would have required the School of Engineering to shoehorn all its instruction into two years of training—a practical impossibility.[43]

In the end, the Peabody Report became a dead letter. Instead of adopting it, the board of trustees created a presidents council to advise it in the reorganization process. This council was dominated by an alliance between President Critz and Chancellor Alfred Hume of the University of Mississippi, both of whom wished to kill the reorganization idea. The board had earlier eliminated the programs in Electrical Engineering and Mechanical Engineering at the University of Mississippi, leaving it with only Civil Engineering, and Hume wanted his lost departments back. In 1933, he addressed the board of trustees, arguing that no Mississippi student should be prevented from attending the university and appreciating its atmosphere, regardless of the course of study he or she wished to follow. He boasted of the university's pioneering efforts to teach agriculture and engineering and criticized what he saw as a "tendency to rob the University, unnecessarily, of some of its own departments, and transfer them to other institutions." He told the board "I do not know that I can stand for that sort of procedure, or "to surrender something that [the university] feels under obligation to hold, or to submit to a kind of dismemberment." Although Critz could not have matched Hume's eloquent address, he undoubtedly shared the chancellor's sentiments. Critz knew that one of the main ideas behind the legislation establishing the land-grant colleges was to create institutions where the "industrial classes" could receive a serious education free from the stultifying atmosphere of the preexisting universities.[44]

The two leaders prevailed, and when the board of trustees assigned roles to the institutions under its jurisdiction it made them broad and overlapping. The board restored the University of Mississippi's Electrical and Mechanical Engineering Departments and made no effort to remove the schools of Science and Business from Mississippi State. In fact, the board's approval of Vice-President A. B. Butts as Director of Instruction at Mississippi State, widely interpreted as approval of an expanded role for the college, led directly to the establishment of a graduate school and the School of Education in 1935. The final threat to institutional existence had been overcome.

CHAPTER FOUR

Toward National Recognition

In spite of the chaos, Mississippi State College made a number of improvements in its programs in the 1930s. Perhaps the most important achievement for the School of Engineering was the establishment of a department of aeronautical engineering. It came into existence in a roundabout way. Various groups had suggested the establishment of an aeronautical engineering department before the 1930s, but the School of Engineering had never acted on the idea. Efforts by the board of trustees to coordinate the offerings of Mississippi's institutions of higher education provided the initial impetus. In 1932, the board issued a vaguely worded directive that Mississippi State consider offering courses in aeronautics. President Critz appointed a special committee to interpret the board's statements, and the committee decided that the board did indeed intend for Mississippi State to set up such a program. The first students were admitted to the program in September 1933. Dean Patterson and the committee apparently hoped that, since the board of trustees had provided the inspiration for aeronautical engineering, the trustees would also provide funding for the new department. They did not, and the new curriculum found itself a home as an orphan of the Department of Mechanical Engineering, classified as a subdivision of the department along with refrigeration and other specialties.

Carpenter was concerned about the prospect of establishing this new curriculum without any meaningful new resources. Aeronautical engineering, he told Critz, has become a "modern and highly specialized branch of Mechanical Engineering, requiring extensive and expensive laboratories and equipment." Georgia Tech had invested over $300,000 in its aeronautical engineering department and then admitted only students who possessed exceptional qualifications. Carpenter was dubious about the proposition of "conferring the bachelor's degree in Aeronautical Engineering from an Engineering School in which there is no organized and equipped department of Aeronautical Engineering headed by a trained and experienced Aeronautical Engineer." To compete successfully with similar departments at other engineering colleges, Carpenter said, required adequate housing, laboratories, and equipment.[1]

Institutional support for aeronautical engineering was not forthcoming either; thus, the new department started with no new money for faculty, housing, or equipment. Its only resources were those it could beg or borrow. The War Department had loaned the college two aircraft, which, though obsolete, could be used for ground instruction. The War Department also provided an old water-cooled airplane engine and several instruments for laboratory work. The lack of an air-cooled radial engine, or an actual flying aircraft, however, made it virtually impossible to teach students the principles of flight or give them practical flight instruction.

Housing posed the most serious problem for the new program. Although plans had been completed for an 11,000-square-foot aeronautics building, no funding materialized. As a temporary measure, the School of Engineering persuaded Professor J. S. Moore, of the Dairy Department, to allow the fledgling department to use the dairy-livestock judging pavilion as a hangar. But the structure was unheated and poorly lighted; moreover, it was still being used for animal shows. Nor could curious visitors be prevented from touching the airplanes, which caused considerable damage. The grain and cattle feed stored in the pavilion attracted rats, which built nests in the airplane wings and chewed on the wood and fabric. Finally, the department had located its engine laboratory inside the foundry, which was unheated and unlighted—making it impossible to hold classes on cold days. To make matters worse, the lack of light made accurate machine work almost impossible.[2]

Staffing the aeronautical engineering subdepartment was a serious problem during the Depression. At first, Dean Patterson thought a retired army or navy officer might be persuaded to head the department free of charge or for a "nominal supplementary salary." Such a person could not be found, however, so Patterson employed Kenneth Withington as an assistant professor in Mechanical Engineering and Sumpter Camp as a flight instructor. Withington held a B.S. degree from Alabama Polytechnical Institute and Camp was a graduate of Mississippi State College who had been taught to fly by Charles Lindbergh. Neither man held an advanced degree; their credentials were based more on enthusiasm for flying than on academic achievements. In 1935, Withington made a half-hearted attempt to take graduate courses in aeronautical engineering. When he found that the universities in which he was interested did not offer summer programs, he tried to find a summer job flying for a commercial airline. The practical experience, he thought, would provide excellent training for his teaching work. Flight instruction took place at the newly established Starkville Municipal Airport west of the city.3

Although the Aeronautical Engineering Department became independent of Mechanical Engineering in 1934, its facilities and funding improved little. "They have certainly labored under difficulties," wrote Patterson in 1936, "not having regular office space, class rooms, and laboratories." Professor Moore probably was sorry he had ever heard of aeronautical engineering, as the department seemed to have no intention of ever moving out of his livestock pavilion. He was "clamoring" for the removal of the airplanes, but no other space was available for them.4

Yet the allure of working with airplanes was attractive to students, and they entered the program in sizable numbers. A poll taken at the end of the Fall 1934 semester showed that many students in both the Schools of Business and Engineering planned to take courses in aeronautics. The explanation for the success of the Aeronautical Engineering Department was largely the department's ability to place its graduates. Even though enrollment had grown dramatically, the department had the highest rate among engineering departments of placing graduates during the Depression.5

In line with the School of Engineering's tradition of providing practical rather than theoretical instruction, the training in Aeronautical Engineering was extremely straightforward. The goal of the program was not to train students in the theory of aerodynamics, but to train engineers who could build airplanes and aircraft engines "on a scientific basis." Thus, the courses available featured such titles as Airplane Welding, Practical Aviation, and

Airplane Structures. By 1938, the department was able to add a course in Advanced Stress Design and, in cooperation with the School of Business, a course in Airline Dispatch and Meteorology.[6]

Besides the establishment of the Department of Aeronautical Engineering, the School of Engineering made significant strides during the 1930s to position itself for future growth. One of the most hotly debated issues in Mississippi in the mid-1930s was the desirability of persuading industries to move to the state. Though vigorously opposed by traditionalists who could imagine nothing other than an agrarian, cotton-dependent Mississippi, support for schemes intended to entice industry to Mississippi had strengthened in many areas of the state. After vigorous debate, the Mississippi legislature passed an act in 1936 officially inaugurating the industrial initiative: The Balance Agriculture with Industry Act, or BAWI. The act was written so as to promote industrialization in Mississippi by allowing communities to sell bonds intended to provide incentives for industries to locate in the state.[7]

The faculty of the School of Engineering, who had long been encouraging increased industrialization in Mississippi, were in complete accord with the goals of BAWI. President George Duke Humphrey, who replaced Critz, was asked to describe what the college could do to promote the BAWI program. He, in turn, asked Professor Ernest L. Lucas, of the Department of Mechanical Engineering, to study the possibility of establishing a department of industrial engineering to train managers for the factories that the BAWI initiative was supposed to lure to Mississippi. Lucas concluded that the need was great, and that if Mississippi was to succeed in the BAWI program, trained men were needed to supervise plants. The curriculum he recommended included seventy-two semester hours of course work that combined business management and engineering. Although he lacked an advanced degree, Lucas offered himself as a candidate for the headship of the department if it were established; but funds to begin a free-standing program in the School of Engineering were not available. As a partial response to the need for additional people trained in industrial management, the Department of Mechanical Engineering further subdivided itself so that students entering in 1939 could choose either a power machinery or an industrial option.[8]

Although establishment of the Aeronautical Engineering Department and the Industrial Engineering option reflected a desire to keep abreast of new developments in technology and industrial organization, the new programs actually were hollow shells. Both programs had been established with little or no new investment in facilities, faculty, or equipment. The Aeronautical Engineering Department was an example of the phenomenon of organizing new programs without the resources to operate them in a legitimate, professional way. As described above, from the beginning, courses were taught in a dairy barn by inexperienced faculty members without advanced degrees using borrowed, obsolete equipment.

Students who trust the assurances in college catalogs usually are the last to appreciate deficiencies in their academic programs, and these were no exception. They continued to enroll in large numbers despite the strained resources of the institution. Enrollment rose from 923 in 1933-34 to 2,698 in 1940-41 with the most dramatic increase occurring between the 1935-36 and the 1937-38 sessions. About half the students were in the School of Engineering. From one point of view, this increase in enrollment was a good thing—it showed that Mississippi's economic health was improving. From another point of view, the enrollment figures were bad news for Mississippi State College. Appropriations did not increase along with enrollment, and the School of Engineering, along with the rest of the college, had to educate more students with what were essentially declining funds. As President Humphrey noted in his biennial report of 1937, appropriations had not changed between 1932 and 1937, although there had been an increase of more than 100 percent in enrollment.[9]

Some departments were in more desperate straits. During the late 1930s, for example, Civil Engineering operated on a budget that was less than it had received in 1911. Although the department offered a course in hydraulics, it had no hydraulics apparatus—a situation, wrote Dewey McCain, analogous to an English instructor telling his students, "Now if we had a pen and paper, this is the method you would use to write . . . a report." One way of economizing, McCain wrote, was to eliminate the testing of construction materials for industry. To do so, however, would be "a confession of less than mediocrity that I do not want to make."[10]

Pressures on the School of Engineering created by increased enrollment, coupled with stable or declining resources, were exacerbated by the changes taking place in the engineering profession at the regional and national levels. From the earliest days, engineering education in the United States has been torn between two concepts—the "shop culture" view and the view of the engineer as a professional. Proponents of the "shop culture" viewpoint argue

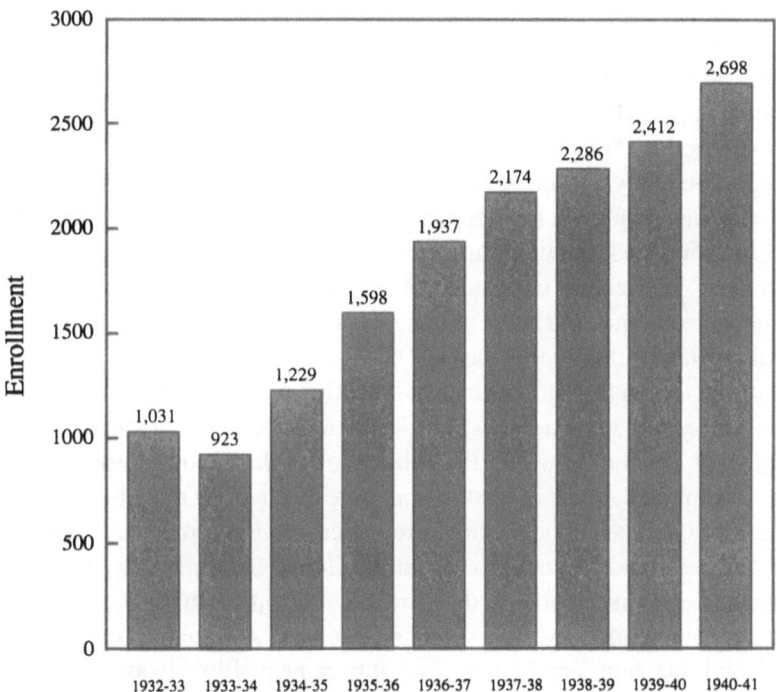

Student Enrollment, 1933-1941

that the engineer should be taught to perform the basic processes involved in manufacturing, insisting that engineers should be trained in the shop where they could acquire skills in woodworking, metalcasting, and machining. Opponents of shop-based education argue that the engineer should view himself or herself as a professional person, not as a tradesman. They have fought for the establishment of an engineering curriculum based on theoretical studies that deemphasize shop work. Instead, they support a curriculum concentrating on the study of mathematics and the basic sciences, complemented by a strong grounding in the liberal arts.[11]

Throughout its history the School of Engineering at Mississippi State College had been firmly committed to the ideal of the shop oriented engineer. Even though its catalogs and other documents referred to the theoretical content of engineering courses, in practice the word *theory* usually referred to how machines and equipment worked, rather than to the scientific principles underlying fundamental processes. In general, the school used the kinds of teaching methods criticized by William E. Wickenden, an engineer who had held faculty appointments at the University of Wisconsin and MIT, along with several executive positions in industry. The Schools produce "engineering students who devote comparatively little time to reflective study and thought," Wickenden reported, "[they] do no collateral reading and pursue no independent inquiries out of pure interest, being kept busy in grinding out innumerable, small-dimensioned set tasks." Such graduates, Wickenden concluded, were "industrious, proficient in a conventional technique, but stale, unimaginative, lacking in scientific grasp and devoid of intellectual enthusiasms."[12]

During the 1930s the engineering profession was attempting redefine itself. Its leaders were taking steps similar to those that lent structure to the medical profession following the publication of the Flexner Report in 1910. The recommendations of that report had resulted in the elimination of dozens of medical schools and led to the creation of a medical curriculum that became standardized throughout the United States. By the 1920s most states had established standards for medical licensure that were essentially those recommended by the American Medical Association's Council on Medical Education. For the first time, it became possible to assume that the holder of a medical degree had mastered a body of knowledge that was similar in content regardless of where the physician had earned a medical degree.[13]

In several ways the situation of the nation's engineering schools in 1930 paralleled that of the medical schools two decades earlier. Until the publication of the Flexner Report and the subsequent development of standardized curricula, medical education was marked by extraordinary diversity. Although the United States had some excellent medical schools, it also had many that were so weak as to be hardly deserving of the name. The best medical schools were typified by Johns Hopkins, an institution that viewed medical education as inseparable from scientific research and the basic sciences. Carefully selected students spent their first two years in the classroom and laboratory, dealing with patients in the hospital or "practicing" (in any sense of the word) only during their last two years in attendance. Hopkins "stood for a new synthesis of medicine and the larger culture." The weaker university medical schools and the proprietary institutions, on the other hand, had minimal entrance requirements, few laboratories and libraries, and nonexistent research programs. Each state set its own licensing requirements, which in states like Mississippi meant that there were no requirements. The impact of the Flexner Report, therefore, lay in the willingness of state medical boards to adopt the recommendations of the Council on Medical Education, which, in effect, made it a national accreditation agency.[14]

In the early part of this century, schools of engineering varied from one another in much the same way that medical schools did. Rensselaer Polytechnic Institute—along with Cornell, The Massachusetts Institute of Technology, and The California Institute of Technology—occupied a place in engineering education comparable to that of Johns Hopkins in medicine. They were followed by second- and third-rank colleges and universities and a host of small proprietary schools, sometimes known as "foremen's schools." Even these were not at the bottom of the barrel, however. In the late 1920s, the American Association of Engineers moved to eradicate correspondence schools in engineering, which it thought were "springing up, like mushrooms, all over the country." Buz Walker had enthusiastically approved of this effort to "wipe out the 'Educational Demi Monde,'" which he thought existed to "fleece the innocent student, the young man who has ambition and is trying to rise in the world, out of his money."[15]

In 1923, the American Society for Engineering Education commissioned William Wickenden to direct a study of engineering education in the United States and suggest ways in which to better standardize it. The study was undertaken specifically to reshape engineering education in the same way the Flexner Report had transformed medical education. Leaders in engineering education could see that "following radical change in educational policy, [medical education] enjoyed enlarged public recognition and financial support." In the same way that it had provided financial support for the Flexner Report, the Carnegie Foundation supplied a grant to underwrite the costs of the study.[16]

By 1932, thirty different states had established standards for licensing engineers. No single state's requirements, however, were comprehensive enough to serve as a national model. To provide some form of national direction for engineering education, the Engineers' Council for Professional Development (ECPD) appointed a Committee on Engineering Schools (later known as the Education and Accrediting Committee), "to formulate criteria for colleges of engineering which will insure to their graduates a sound educational background for practicing the engineering profession." Inclusion on the ECPD's list of accredited institutions soon became recognized nationwide as a valid indicator of quality in engineering education in the same way that the AMA's list of accredited institutions had come to dominate medical education.[17]

While the ECPD shared the AMA's goal of ensuring a high level of professional education, its philosophy differed in several important ways from that of the AMA. First, the ECPD examined engineering programs within institutions on an individual basis. This meant that each engineering discipline was examined separately, that some would be fully accredited while others were not. The ECPD wanted to avoid the all-or-nothing accreditation system used by the AMA. It promised to withhold accreditation only from those curricula "which omit a significant portion of a subject in which the public may reasonably expect engineers of that field to have competence." Second, the ECPD avoided setting universal, monolithic standards, such as the AMA's, instead encouraging experimentation in engineering curricula in order to prevent "ossification." Third, the ECPD promised to consider both qualitative and quantitative factors in its inspections. Qualitative criteria, which were particularly important, focused on such factors as a faculty's qualifications, experience, intellectual interests, and professional productivity. Also included was an examination of the quality of scientific (and other) departments, in which engineering students received instruction, as well as the attitude of the administration toward teaching, research, and scholarly production.[18]

Unfortunately, the School of Engineering at Mississippi State College did not take the ECPD's statement of goals very seriously, or it did not think the ECPD would apply it rigorously. In 1937, the school applied for accreditation, apparently without much thought or discussion. Dean Patterson possessed a copy of the Wickenden Report, which he later donated to the Mississippi State University Library. The underlining and marginalia in his copy of the "Summary of Results" appears to support the idea that he did not pay much attention to the report's most fundamental conclusions. After surviving the blows of the early 1930s, the School of Engineering had developed a complacent attitude, in part because, by 1937, it was the third largest school of engineering in the South behind Georgia Tech and LSU, even though this meant that "space [was] crowded beyond saturation." In addition, the school had long operated on the assumption that it was held in high esteem throughout the country as long as its graduates could readily obtain jobs.[19]

The evaluators sent by the Engineers' Council for Professional Development did not share this opinion, which meant that the ECPD's inspection proved devastating for the School of Engineering. The ECPD issued a report "condemnatory" of the School of Engineering and refused to grant accreditation to any of the departments.[20] Salaries were too low, the ECPD told the School of Engineering; class sections were too big; teaching loads were too high. Laboratories, space, and equipment were inadequate. And, finally, the faculty was too inbred, lacking in advanced degrees and research productivity. The ECPD also criticized the college's practice of holding its faculty members responsible for the operation of institutional utilities as well as for teaching, a duty which traditionally consumed much of the time available to the mechanical and electrical engineers. In essence the ECPD told the School of Engineering that if it wished its accreditation to rank favorably with that of other engineering colleges, it would have to undertake a wholesale revision of its organization, personnel, and educational philosophy. The ECPD inspection, thought A. G. Holmes, marked the "end of innocence" for the "parochial" engineering faculty.[21]

The impact of the ECPD's inspection of engineering schools in the 1930s cannot be overestimated. Although 62 percent of the nation's engineering schools were ranked in the "high" category, which meant that the great majority of their programs met at least minimal standards, the rest found that few or none of their programs met the ECPD's standards. They were in the same situation as the marginal medical schools that had failed to meet the AMA's standards two decades earlier. They either had to improve or go out of business.[22]

The devastating effect of the loss of accreditation in the aftermath of the Bilbo firings was fresh in the minds of most faculty members, and a repeat of such an experience was unthinkable. Mississippi State College determined to fight back and gain accreditation. The most basic problem for the school had always been a lack of funding with which to employ well-trained faculty members and purchase equipment. President Humphrey was acutely aware of the College's overall funding crisis. Walker and Humphrey were the only presidents Mississippi State College had ever had who spent much time in stronger institutions of higher education. Humphrey seemed particularly embarrassed by the failure of the School of Engineering to gain accreditation. He asked the legislature for a special appropriation for the School of Engineering and received a special $15,000 allotment from the State Building Commission to use for new equipment, which was about half of what had been originally requested. Joy over this meager appropriation was diminished by the behavior of the college's Budget Committee. Unaware that the Building Commission had prohibited the School of Engineering from spending any of the new money on consumable supplies or labor, it assumed that the School of Engineering could use its windfall for operating expenses and drastically cut the engineering school's operating funds, which further weakened its position. The level to which the school had fallen became clear when the Mechanical Engineering Department made room for its new equipment in the steam laboratory. In 1939-1940, for example, the faculty removed engines from the laboratory that were nearly as old as the school itself (one engine had been displayed at the St. Louis World's fair in 1904, whereas the newest engine was purchased in 1925).[23]

One of the main criticisms of the ECPD inspection team concerned the experience and expertise of the engineering faculty. Since the School of Engineering had not been able to compete for faculty members on a national or regional level since its earliest days, nearly all of the engineering faculty members were Mississippi State College graduates who had decided to teach at the institution for personal reasons. Few of them possessed advanced degrees, although most had taken a few summer graduate courses. Of all the faculty members employed between 1902 and 1937 in the Mechanical Engineering Department, only one, Albert Barnes, held any degree higher than the B.S., and President Hardy had fired him in 1910. Several, including associate professors Earl E. Cooley, Ernest L. Lucas, and Osmond D. M. Varnado, had spent some time trying to complete master's degrees during their summer vacations but with little progress. It was clear that accreditation would not be forthcoming if the faculty were not somehow substantially upgraded.[24]

The most glaring example of academic inbreeding and inadequate academic credentials was the venerable Randle Churchill Carpenter, who had been associated with the institution for nearly forty years. Carpenter had received his bachelor of science degree from Mississippi A & M in 1895 and immediately joined the instructional staff. Although he possessed no advanced degree, he became head of the department in 1912. The ECPD inspection team apparently had been clear in their recommendation that the highest-ranking members of the faculty should possess advanced degrees, which meant that Carpenter and several of his colleagues would have to leave the faculty before accreditation would be granted.

In a way, this was a blessing in disguise for the institution, because it provided a perfect excuse for separating campus services from the academic engineering departments. Accordingly, Carpenter was made the director of a unified campus services department and given the title professor emeritus, although President Humphrey made it clear to the board of trustees that he would have no voice in operating the department. In spite of his long experience, Carpenter seemed afraid that he might be dismissed from the college and was effusive in his gratitude to Patterson, Humphrey, and the board of trustees for finding him a new position.[25] He was joined in the new department of utilities, Buildings and Grounds by Earl Cooley, another Mississippi State College graduate who lacked an advanced degree. Indeed, Carpenter's apprehension had not been without foundation. In 1938, several members of the board of trustees became angry when they learned that he was heavily involved both in operating an ice plant in West Point and in outside consulting. They decided that Carpenter's participation in these outside business activities meant there was not enough work involved in supervising the campus services for two men, and they forced the college to let him go. The woodworking shop, which had been an anachronism in the Mechanical Engineering Department for many years, was finally done away with by transferring it to the Industrial Education Department. W. B. Montgomery, another product of inbreeding, went with it.[26]

Humphrey planned to fill the vacancies thus created by "imported men" whose presence, he hoped, would deflect ECPD criticism about inbreeding. A. G. Holmes, an engineer who had earned bachelor's degrees at Clemson and Cornell and a master's degree at the University of Michigan, replaced Carpenter as head of the Mechanical Engineering Department; several other faculty members whose first degree was not from Mississippi State were hired. Existing staff members without advanced degrees were encouraged to pursue them and all but one found themselves taking graduate courses in the summer of 1939.[27]

The final major change resulting from the ECPD's inspection trip was the beginning of a research program. Research had never been part of faculty life at Mississippi State, largely because the institution had always been so poorly funded that faculty members barely had enough hours in a day to attend to their teaching duties, and because salaries had never been adequate to attract faculty members with advanced degrees and research experience. Yet, as Dewey McCain reported in 1938, every accrediting group had asked the school to explain, "What contribution have you made to the profession; How many papers, bulletins or books have you published?"[28] Such concerns were far from new. From time to time, department heads and deans had pointed out that the college would be taken seriously by the engineering profession only if the faculty were given the opportunity to contribute to the creation of knowledge. "When the time comes that we have the time and equipment for experimental work in engineering," wrote Civil Engineer Robert Gay in 1918, "then we will be able to take our place before the people of the community as doing something worthy of recognition." "Engineering reputation," he continued, "is rarely gained through the routine class work of instruction; but comes through the contribution of engineering science to something of value."[29]

Pleas such as this fell on deaf ears. After all, among all the presidents Mississippi State College had ever had, only Walker had engaged in serious scholarship of any kind, and his scholarly career had ended with his dissertation work. Also, it is not clear that the leadership of the engineering departments really understood what scholarly research was. In 1938, for example, McCain told President Humphrey that "the job of a teacher is to teach, and that he is being paid for that job; not for the amount of publicity he can get."[30] McCain used the word publicity as a synonym for the publication of scholarly research and seemed to think that the publication of research results was more or less equivalent to making one's self the subject of newspaper articles or giving talks to public audiences. A final impediment to research was the attitude of Starkville businessmen who objected to faculty members engaging in any kind of activity that seemed to compete with them. Political pressure from the business community was sufficient to prevent faculty members from engaging in consulting work.[31]

The employment of A. G. Holmes, who understood that the publication of research results would "enhance the reputation of the school and of the college," was motivated partially by the desire to initiate a modest research program. In his first report to President Humphrey he recommended that "research projects should be started by each staff member."[32] In truth, though, even if a president, dean, or department head had wished to encourage faculty research in engineering, most theoretical approaches to engineering problems would have been all but impossible because of the general absence of graduate training among the engineering faculty.

Service-oriented research devoted to the solution of practical, local problems certainly would have been feasible if adequate administrative and financial support had been available. Since the late nineteenth century the faculty had hoped for the establishment of a federal engineering experiment station program organized along the lines of the agricultural experiment station system. In the hopeful days of early 1929, Dean Moody urged President Walker to request a $150,000 building from the state to house a materials-testing laboratory to house the federal engineering experiment station he thought would soon be a reality. The Depression put these hopes on hold and only the entrance of the United States into World War II revived hopes for federal funding. Accordingly, President Humphrey asked the board of trustees to authorize the establishment of an engineering experiment station which would "begin work in a small way."33

Although the board authorized the Engineering Experiment Station in January 1941, wartime pressures made it highly impractical for the institution to embark on new ventures, and the station did not become a reality until 1944. Its original mission was extremely practical. Essentially it revolved around cooperating with the Agricultural Experiment Station to "determine new or more economical uses for the natural resources of the state as they apply to engineering and industry." The Engineering Experiment Station was also to complete low-cost studies for state agencies and industries at no charge, or at a nominal cost.34

The slow movement toward excellence in engineering education was halted by the entry of the United States into World War II. Faculty members and students left *en masse*. As happened during World War I, the resources of the School of Engineering were in large part devoted to special war-related training programs sponsored by the War Department. During the war, the School of Engineering participated in several different programs operated by colleges and universities under the supervision of the Office of Education. In 1940-41, the programs were known as Engineering Defense Training (EDT), in 1941-42 as Engineering, Science, and Management Defense Training (ESMDT), and from 1942-45 as Engineering, Science, and Management War Training (ESMWT). Altogether some 7,300 students participated in these special training programs designed to provide American industry with technically trained professionals. In addition, the School of

Engineering administered the Vocational Defense Training Program which trained skilled workmen. A radio school trained men to repair radios, and others were trained in welding, machining, foundry, patternmaking, and drafting. The Army Air Force selected Mississippi State College as a site for a unit of the Army Air Force College Training Program which provided basic education for pilots, navigators and bombardiers. Although the five-month program consisted mainly of such subjects as mathematics, physics, English, history, and geography, it absorbed most of the energies of Sumpter Camp, who had become acting head of the Aeronautical Engineering Department. In 1943, the college became home to a unit of the Army Specialized Training Program, directed by Dean Patterson. Depending on their previous training, students were taught the rudiments of civil, electrical, or mechanical engineering.[35]

By far the most important war-related program for the School of Engineering was a series of educational programs designed to increase American industrial production. Although the United States was not at war in 1940, the conflict in Europe and Asia sufficiently alarmed Congress for it to take modest steps to prepare the country for a potential emergency. The initial EDT program had two main purposes. The first was to provide the rudiments of a technical education to men who could fill vacancies in defense-related industries and government; the second was to assist in recovery from the Depression. At first, unemployed men could apply for the training program, which offered excellent prospects for employment.[36]

The School of Engineering proposed to offer five courses in the EDT program including production engineering, engineering drafting, materials inspection and testing, tool engineering, and aircraft structures. They were to start in January 1941 and were to last twelve weeks, during which time students would receive around 500 hours of instruction.[37] Of these courses engineering drafting, production engineering, and materials inspection and testing attracted enough students to be offered, although the production engineering course was only grudgingly approved by the Office of Education because of low enrollment. Vocational training, thought Dean Patterson, was a much more promising enterprise.[38]

The second phase of the training program was more ambitious and focused. Whereas the prewar EDT program was designed to satisfy a vaguely perceived shortage of engineers possessing training in defense-related areas, the ESMDT program reflected a national shortage of trained physical scientists and production supervisors. Land-grant institutions were asked to operate these management training programs because of their similarity to the general noncredit, off-campus agricultural extension work that the institutions were used to conducting. Underlying the program was the realization that the United States had an inadequate number of competent engineers, chemists, physicists, and production supervisors to operate war-related industries effectively. The crash program was designed to remedy this shortage by matching faculty members with people already employed in war-related industries. Faculty members experienced in teaching engineering, chemistry, physics, and business management served as "educational supervisors," while the actual teaching of the courses was done by individuals already employed in the war industry.[39]

Most members of the engineering faculty participated in the program as educational advisors. Because of the extra pay involved, they found the experience quite agreeable. Involvement of the engineering faculty—who, of course, were employees of the state—in a federally funded program was a new experience; but the financial arrangements posed a problem for them. Faculty members had never received supplemental compensation when asked to perform extra duties for the college. In fact, it would have been impossible before the war to pay faculty members overtime because no standard workweek had ever been established. President Humphrey seemed reluctant to establish a clearly defined workweek or to set a precedent for overtime compensation. The board of trustees also seemed hesitant to allow faculty members to earn supplemental salaries. Some in the administration thought faculty members should be required to work overtime without additional compensation or to accept a reduction in their contractual salaries, then use the ESMDT funds to return them to the established level. As Dean Patterson pointed out, both options were objectionable to the faculty. No faculty member wanted to perform extra work for nothing. They realized that it would be foolhardy to accept a cut in their contractual salaries and then hope that enough courses would be funded to make up the difference. Also, many feared that the administration would refuse to restore the old salary levels once the war emergency ended. President Humphrey accepted these arguments and agreed to establish a standard workweek of 41.5 hours and to allow faculty members to receive ESMDT salaries on an overtime basis. This decision allowed all members of the engineering faculty to receive salary supplements, although, because of the extremely low salaries faculty members already received, their hourly rate was comparable to the wages received by tradesmen recently graduated from the college's Vocational Defense Training School.[40]

As was the case during World War I, World War II thoroughly disrupted ordinary engineering education. The traditional student all but disappeared as enlistments and the draft took their toll. From a prewar high of 2,327 in 1939-40, enrollment declined to 1,997 at the beginning of the 1942 academic year and to 917 by year's end. Only 404 students enrolled in 1944-45. Whereas the enrollment in 1939-40 had been almost 900 students higher than the University of Mississippi, the 1944-45 enrollment was more than 300 fewer, reflecting Mississippi State's predominantly male clientele. Initially, the School of Engineering fared better than its sister schools because the Selective Service had recommended the deferment of engineering students. Nevertheless, by 1944, enrollment had shrunk to such an extent that only twenty-one students received degrees (the same number that had graduated in 1902). Six of these were from the School of Engineering.[41]

The engineering faculty was disrupted by the pressures of war. Those with engineering degrees were much in demand by the armed forces and war-related industries. Consequently, the School of Engineering experienced massive departures of faculty members. By 1944, only a skeleton staff remained. Kenneth Withington had joined the Army and Sumpter Camp was engaged full-time in flight training. This left only one instructor—T. S. Edwards. Civil Engineering had dropped to two instructors, with one of them scheduled to be drafted. Electrical Engineering had four available for instruction, including Dean Patterson; but two were in danger of being drafted. Mechanical Engineering was down to Holmes and Varnado (who was also on the verge of departure). Only the Drawing Department, with three of four faculty members available for teaching duties, had remained near its pre-war size. In one way, this was a liability—because of the decreased civilian enrollment and the abrupt termination of the war-training programs and elimination of student deferments for engineers in 1944, Patterson faced the possibility of having to fire faculty members who were deemed superfluous. With a tiny student body and a demoralized and uncertain faculty, Humphrey predicted that "the most difficult year in the history of the College [is] ahead."[42]

Chapter Five

The Birth of a Modern College

The enormous disruptions caused by World War II in Mississippi higher education inspired the board of trustees to engage in a round of institutional soul-searching that was more serious than anything that had been attempted since the Peabody survey of 1933. In the summer of 1944 the board had just become a constitutionally protected body which meant that it possessed a kind of political freedom unknown to previous boards. Indeed, the time was auspicious for another investigation of the nature of the institutions which had been entrusted to the board. Enrollment had fallen so dramatically throughout the state that few students would have been affected by reorganization, and so many faculty members had left the campuses during the war that reorganization of the faculties could have taken place in a relatively painless manner through the process of rehiring. Finally, much of the buildings, facilities, and equipment belonging to the seven institutions had fallen into such a state of disrepair that a redirection of new funds would have gone far toward achieving reorganization.[1]

Thus, in October 1944 the board employed Joseph E. Gibson, the Director of Higher Education of the Louisiana State Department of Education, to head a commission to study the seven institutions under the jurisdiction of the board and provide it with suggestions for strengthening higher education in Mississippi. The commission submitted its report in August 1945, recommending a series of changes designed to dramatically transform higher education in Mississippi by strengthening the University of Mississippi and weakening the other institutions in the state. Although the reconstituted board of trustees was no longer a pawn of Mississippi's governors, it remained a highly political body. Its members were committed to protecting the interests of certain institutions. An unofficial list of priorities of long standing placed the University of Mississippi at the head of the class of institutions of higher learning and Mississippi State second. Thus, although the consultants who wrote the report did not despise the principles underlying land-grant education as much as their predecessors who had conducted the O'Shea and Peabody surveys, they cared little for the land-grant ideal of educating the children of the industrial classes. Probably this was due to the influence of H. M. Ivy who headed the "Ole Miss faction" on the board of trustees from 1944 to 1956 and who wanted to keep all other state institutions as small, impoverished, and specialized as possible.[2] Undoubtedly, Ivy, who chaired the board committee that supervised the study, exerted considerable influence on the selection of consultants and the tone of the report. Indeed, one of the few major recommendations in the report that could not have been drawn from a University of Mississippi "wish list" was the abolition of the School of Engineering at the University of Mississippi, and the transfer of its programs to Mississippi State. Apparently, discontinuation of the University of Mississippi's School of Engineering was a topic of some discussion among the faculty of Mississippi State. Knowing that the likelihood of the board forcing the University of Mississippi to eliminate its engineering school was next to zero, Dean Patterson, in his 1944-45 report to President Humphrey, facetiously welcomed its Dean, Lee H. Johnson, as an assistant dean at Mississippi State.[3]

The School of Engineering at the University of Mississippi was never abolished, of course, and the impact of the Gibson Report was modest. The blatant political bias of the report, coupled with the influx of veterans into the state's institutions of higher learning, made it all but impossible for the board of trustees to implement many of the report's recommendations, particularly those having to do with the reallocation of programs and services. Yet, the process of collecting information and preparing an institutional response to the requests of the consultants proved a valuable experience for the School. The main value of studies such as that conducted by Joseph Gibson's committee often lies in the necessity for individual units to examine themselves in detail and identify their strengths and weaknesses. That was the case with the School of Engineering which was at a turning point in its history.

In spite of the difficulties he faced while presiding over Mississippi State during the late 1930s and the war years, President Humphrey retained a great sense of optimism regarding Mississippi State and the State of Mississippi. A chief objective of the college, he told the new board of trustees during its second meeting in July 1944, was improvement of the income of the people of Mississippi which would then improve the "social, educational, moral, and religious conditions" of the state. This meant that Mississippi State "whose primary purpose [is] to promote the interests of the agricultural and industrial classes, will be more responsible than any other educational institution in the state for postwar planning and development." A modernized School of Engineering played a major role in Humphrey's plans which gave it a dramatically expanded role. By 1937 he had already gained board approval for a department of ceramic engineering which was supposed to find new commercial uses for the ubiquitous clays which perhaps are Mississippi's most abundant natural resource. To meet the postwar needs of the people of Mississippi, he thought, full-scale departments of aeronautical, architectural, petroleum, and chemical engineering that could gain ECPD accreditation were needed. The board approved Humphrey's recommendations on the same day that he made them and authorized Mississippi State to put these programs into operation "as the needs arise and facilities permit."[4]

The faculty of the School of Engineering was less confident about the future than President Humphrey. During the course of the Gibson study, Dean Patterson had appointed a committee composed of Professors McCain, Holmes, and Associate Professor Henry P. Neal to make several recommendations concerning the future of engineering education at Mississippi State. In essence, the direction recommended by the Holmes committee was a very conservative one shaped by the experience of chronic underfunding. Mississippi State, the committee argued, should abandon its attempts to develop a full-scale School of Engineering and instead concentrate on civil, electrical, and mechanical engineering with all other branches, including aeronautical engineering, existing as subsidiaries of one of the three main departments. It recommended that aeronautical engineering should be a branch of mechanical engineering, and architectural engineering should be under civil engineering. Chemical and petroleum engineering should be left in the School of Science. If the three major departments were to maintain a minimum level of quality that would allow them to pass accreditation inspections, teaching loads would have to be reduced to reasonable levels, all departments should be expected to engage in research, and maximum prewar enrollments could not be greatly exceeded. In addition, the Committee recommended, significant sums for new equipment as well as additional faculty members and graduate assistants, were needed to upgrade the three major branches.5

Although the School of Engineering had throughout its history been devoted almost entirely to instruction, Holmes and his colleagues argued that the time had come to reexamine that role. They agreed with Humphrey that, besides providing instruction in the fundamentals of engineering, the school should also be responsible for contributing to the economic and social development of Mississippi and to the common store of engineering knowledge. For the first time the school officially recognized that teaching and research were part of the same overall fabric of academic excellence. As long as the engineering faculty did not contribute anything to the store of engineering knowledge, the Committee wrote, the faculty would be "professionally, parasites."6

A companion report prepared a few months later again emphasized the importance of engineering research. Dewey McCain had become assistant director of the Engineering Experiment Station in 1944, largely because of his success in obtaining the first externally funded research award in the history of the school. (The dean automatically served as director.) McCain had obtained a small contract from the Tennessee Valley Authority in 1944 to study "Wood Joints made with Nails in Drilled Holes." No one in the School of Engineering had ever done contract research before, and there was little institutional understanding of how valuable such work could be. It was an enlightening experience for McCain who was surprised to realize that after working on the project for six months he had accumulated supplies and equipment worth more than the amount the Research and Experiment Station had spent on the project. His experience led him to recommend a much-expanded role for research in the School of Engineering.7

McCain's thinking had evolved considerably since 1938 when he had equated scholarly publication with publicity-seeking, and he had come to understand that there was "no sharp dividing line . . . between research and instruction [or] . . . between fundamental and end research." The first step in developing an engineering research program, he thought, was to establish a political constituency that would support engineering research in the same way that agriculture's various constituencies supported its research. By "preaching the partnership of education and industry," McCain said, businessmen and manufacturers could be convinced that sustained effort in engineering research would pay significant dividends to the state. People must be led to understand that the colleges's research activities had to be both practical and visionary, but not overly practical or visionary. "Possibly we should say first what a research laboratory is not," he wrote. "It is not a testing laboratory. It is not a trouble-shooting shop. It is not a plaything for the theorist to dabble in." Such an operation, he thought, could start from fairly modest beginnings. Smaller laboratories often had been able to do notable work and many valuable contributions originated in modest facilities. An initial investment of $10,000 would be enough to get the program off the ground and, although initial state support was essential, the possibility of federal support was quite real.[8]

Patterson agreed with the work of the Holmes committee and recommended the adoption of its conclusions. In most respects, the consultants who wrote the report on the School of Engineering for the Gibson report agreed with the school's senior faculty. Although the consultants did not take individual responsibility for the sections they wrote, the person responsible for the portion of the report on engineering was probably Paul W. Chapman, dean of the School of Agriculture at the University of Georgia. As we have seen, the committee had been created in part to enhance the interests of the University of Mississippi, and none of the other twenty-four consultants and assistants had any recognizable identification with land-grant education in general or with engineering education in particular. Chapman agreed that sizable amounts of new money were needed to purchase equipment and employ new faculty members if the school were to become competitive. He also agreed that the School of Engineering should begin to emphasize research. There was little doubt, his report concluded, that Mississippi's greatest need was a better balance between agriculture and industry, and that the Engineering Experiment Station could perform an important role in helping Mississippi develop industrially. The "state cannot afford to support technical research designed to make discoveries in the field of engineering," the report continued; but it could have an impact on Mississippi's develop-

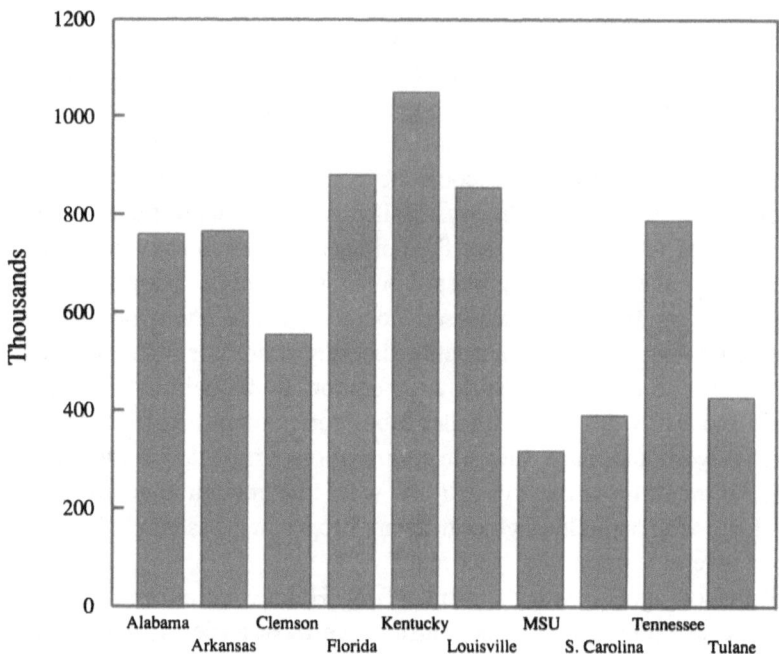

Total Value of Buildings and Equipment, Departments of Engineering at Selected Southern Universities, circa 1945. Annual Report, *1945*, p. 10.

ment by helping industries identify and exploit Mississippi's natural resources. Chapman rejected the conclusions of the Holmes Committee that the school should return to the basics. Like Humphrey, he urged the board to provide funding for programs in petroleum, aeronautical, and architectural engineering which would make it correspond more closely to other schools of engineering in the South.[9]

World War II sharply illustrated the nation's need for trained technical professionals, and the curriculum in engineering education once again came under intense national scrutiny. Throughout the history of engineering education a conflict has raged between those who believe that the curriculum should focus on technical and professional subjects and those who think that engineering students should receive an education based on science and mathematics including serious study in the other liberal arts. Those favoring the first point of view argue that it is impossible to avoid the unending

Stephen D. Lee (c. 1900), first
president of Mississippi A & M

Charles Edgar Ard (c. 1901), professor
of mechanic arts and electricity

The Academic Building, c. 1882

A. J. Weichardt (c. 1901), professor of mechanic arts

Buz Walker (c. 1902), director of the school of engineering, 1902-1925, and president of Mississippi A & M, 1925-1930

Forge Shop, 1886

Foundry, 1886

Machine Workshop, 1886

Carpentry and Wood Turning Shop, 1886

Students using line-shaft equipment in the Mechanical Engineering Machine Shop, c. 1910

Above: John Crumpton Hardy (c. 1910), third president of Mississippi A & M; *right*: students in agricultural engineering just before World War I

The Engineering Building, c. 1915, built by Professors Ard and Barnes

Left: Students in civil engineering, 1915; *above*: Howard W. Moody (c. 1926), dean of engineering, 1925-1930

Mechanic arts equipment, 1915

Electrical Engineering Laboratory, 1927

Mechanical Engineering Machine Shop, c. 1930

Dewey M. McCain (1943), professor of civil engineering

Kenneth Withington (1940), professor of aeronautical engineering

Matthew Livingston Freeman (1940), professor of drawing

A. G. Holmes (1940), professor of mechanical engineering

Right: L. L. Patterson (c. 1945), dean of engineering, 1930-1949; *below*: students working in the Machine Shop, c. 1950

Above left: August Raspet (c. 1955), director of aerophysics department; *above right*: Harold Flinsch (1950), dean of engineering, 1949-1957; *right*: William Flowers Hand (1926), the founder of advanced studies in chemistry

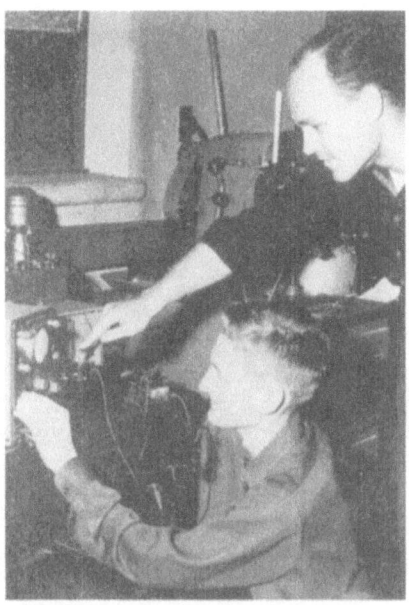

Joseph Cornish, aeronautical engineer (right), and student George Elliott, 1955

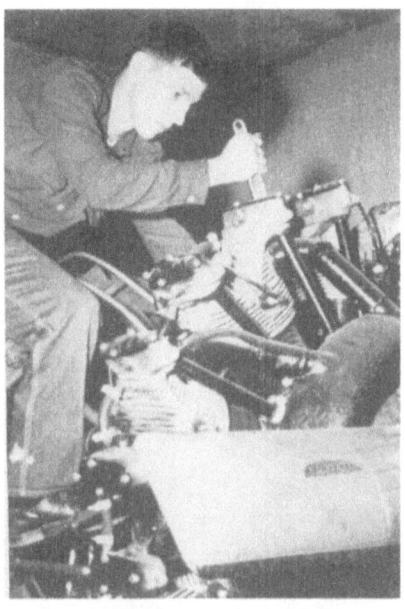

Engine work in the Aerophysics Laboratory, 1955

Machine Shop, Patterson Laboratories, 1951

Above: Students in Power Systems Laboratory, 1957; *right*: Raspet Group Researchers studying airflow by placing tufts on wings and fuselage, 1969

Raspet Flight Research Laboratory, 1992

Aeronautical engineering students working on wind tunnel, 1960

Harry C. Simrall (1958), dean of engineering, 1957-1978

Willie McDaniel (c. 1978), dean of engineering, 1978-1988

An engineering student using a transit, 1979

Robert Altenkirch (1990), dean of engineering, 1988--

Harry Simrall (seated) and engineering professors Willie McDaniel, Larry Hill, and Walter Carnes (left to right), 1975

Walter E. Massey, director of NSF, Joe Thompson, director of NSF Engineering Research Center, and Donald Zacharias, president of Mississippi State University (left to right), at the dedication of the Engineering Research Center, 1990

tendency for engineering problems to become more and more complex. They maintain that if a student is to be able to step from the classroom into a professional position after four years of undergraduate work, he must be required to concentrate on engineering subjects at an early stage and spend nearly all of his undergraduate years studying technical subjects.

Engineering educators favoring the second point of view argue that the purpose of undergraduate education is not to provide a kind of apprenticeship training, but instead to give students a broad understanding of human society. They want the student engineer to emerge from his undergraduate years as a broadly educated professional who, while perhaps not able to solve engineering problems, should be capable of rapidly understanding a wide variety of engineering situations and assuming managerial responsibility.

During its early years the curriculum in engineering education at Mississippi State included a fair number of liberal arts courses. Students were required to take courses in history, government, and economics. Gradually, though, the faculty became convinced that the overriding purpose of the School of Engineering was to prepare students to step into practice immediately, and the curriculum had become more practical in its orientation. The number of nontechnical courses in the curriculum had decreased until by World War II students took only nine semester hours in the humanities and social sciences.[10]

In restricting the curriculum to technical subjects the School of Engineering was swimming against the tide as far as national trends in engineering education were concerned. As they had done in the 1930s leaders in engineering education were vigorously trying to persuade schools of engineering to include more liberal arts courses in their curricula. In 1945, the Committee on Engineering Education of the American Society for Engineering Education recommended that engineering schools follow two fundamental principles in organizing their curricula. First, the committee asked them to build on the recommendations of the Wickenden Report by including a larger amount of nontechnological subject matter and to ensure that required courses were truly basic and fundamental. The "how-to-do courses," said the committee, existed to "enliven the fundamentals and to start our graduates in their professional fields." Second, the committee specifically requested that all engineering schools provide at least 20 percent nontechnical courses in the social studies and humanities.[11]

Thus, in the Fall of 1945, the School of Engineering initiated a study of the curriculum designed to alter it in such a way as to include more of what Patterson called "humanistic-social" courses and more work in the basic sciences and advanced mathematics. Although the changes were far from profound, they did make the curriculum somewhat more scientific and less shop-oriented when they went into effect in 1947. Thirty of 146 semester hours required for graduation were in the humanities and social sciences. Students were required to demonstrate more mathematical ability, as differential calculus, along with analytical geometry was taught as a second-semester freshman course.[12]

The results of this reform varied from department to department. In Aeronautical Engineering, for example, freshmen took physics instead of inorganic chemistry (which was moved to the sophomore year), dropped physical education, and took twelve semester hours of mathematics instead of ten. American Civilization replaced State and County Government. In the sophomore year another history course, World Civilization, replaced English Literature. Courses in plane surveying, slide rule and tool making practices and statics were dropped. In the junior and senior years the curriculum remained focused on courses on the design and fabrication of machines. Yet the movement toward a more theoretical curriculum was visible. Before 1946, the Aeronautical Engineering curriculum had included three required courses that were very much of the how-to variety: Aviation Communication, Airline Dispatching and Meteorology, and Aircraft Welding. In 1946, these courses were replaced by Aircraft Engine Design, Power Plant Components, and an additional course in advanced mathematics. Two elective courses were replaced by two humanities taught by the English Department.[13]

Civil Engineering altered its curriculum as well by joining the other engineering departments in adding more mathematics. World Civilization and Comparative Government replaced a general humanities course. The junior and senior years remained focused on the basic elements of water movement and the design of structures. In the new curriculum, students were given a somewhat more theoretical education with courses such as Concrete Theory replacing Concrete Structures and Fundamentals of Economics and Economics of Industrial Relations replacing the two courses in Highway Economics previously required. The two humanities courses previously taught by the English Department also became part of the curriculum.[14]

Perhaps the most dramatic change in attitude came in the Department of Mechanical Engineering. In 1945 the introduction to the department's courses reiterated its traditional position that the department's role was to teach students to prepare "working drawings and molds, work in forge, foundry, and machine shops, and [gain] familiarity with the operation of power and electric light plants, and the construction of power systems."[15] A year later, however, the Department defined its role more broadly, adopting a more modern definition of the discipline. Mechanical Engineering, the department told its prospective students, was simply that branch of engineering which deals principally with the design, operation, and use of power equipment. Students could choose between two options. The power-machinery option taught students to understand steam power plants, internal combustion engines, heating and air conditioning, thermodynamics, mechanics, and machine design. The industrial-management option taught students to economically use human and physical resources in manufacturing. This program, which marked a major step toward the establishment of a full-scale industrial engineering program, concentrated on industrial organization and management, personnel administration, cost-finding, and time and motion study. In a more remarkable deviation from tradition, the Mechanical Engineering Department clearly told prospective students that the usual technical courses were not sufficient for the professional engineer who needed to be able to move comfortably in nontechnical society. "The consensus of opinion in the field of Engineering," the introduction to the catalog concluded, inadvertently illustrating the point,

> is that curicula [sic] are much to [sic] technical. The Mechanical Engineering Department has varied its curriculum to include courses for the purpose of broadening and liberalizing offerings. This was done to give the student a greater comprehension of those problems which he encounters as a citizen and to try to impress upon him the fact that technical knowledge alone is insufficient to permit him to attain to a more responsible position.

The department then proceeded to divest itself of the last of its cherished shop work. Away went Pattern Making, Plane Surveying, and Forge and

Foundry. No longer did juniors study Machine Tool Practice and Tool Making Practice. Seniors choosing the power-machinery option could graduate without studying welding. In place of these courses came the reforms in the freshman and sophomore years that were shared by the other engineering departments, such as courses in Experimental Engineering. In addition, students were required to take at least one course in the humanities or social sciences in all but one of their eight semesters.[16]

Electrical Engineering perhaps underwent the most dramatic transformation in the 1946 reforms. It had long resisted modernizing its curriculum, even refusing to officially acknowledge the existence of the vacuum tube until World War II. In 1945, it made a small gesture toward reform by adding three courses relating to the communication industry. It added a sophomore course in electronics, a senior-level eight-hour sequence in radio engineering, and a four-semester-hour senior course in telephone engineering. Otherwise, the curriculum remained traditional in the sense that it concentrated on the generation, transmission, and industrial consumption of electrical energy. No humanities or social sciences courses were required, although students were permitted one elective in each of their last two semesters. Given the traditions of the department, it is difficult to imagine advisors recommending anything other than more engineering courses to inquiring students.

In 1946, the Department allowed students to choose from two new options in illumination and industrial electronics which had been added to the traditional power-machinery and communications options. It also added several new courses that reflected the advances in electronics that had taken place during World War II. Courses in Electrical Measurements, Ultra-High Frequency, and Automatic Control complemented the traditional courses. Harry C. Simrall, who matriculated at Mississippi State in 1930 and had been teaching at the institution since 1935, became acting head of the Electrical Engineering Department. Simrall had been instrumental in developing the new option, which was much more theoretical than anything previously available. According to one report, the illumination option was the first of its kind in the South, and the second in the nation.[17]

The final major change in the curriculum that resulted from the postwar reevaluation offerings was the return of Agricultural Engineering to the School of Engineering, becoming a program jointly administered by the School of Agriculture and the School of Engineering. The program that remained in the School of Agriculture was renamed Farm Engineering so as not to cause confusion with the degree curriculum of the School of Engineering. Students in the new engineering program took the same courses as mechanical engineering students for the first two years and then took courses divided between agriculture and engineering during the junior and senior years.[18]

The idea that engineering students should be provided with an eduction that not only gave them training but enabled them to understand society and its workings continued to shape the engineering curriculum at the national level; and the curriculum modifications that had begun in 1946 continued apace. In the introduction to its program in the catalog for 1949-50, for example, the Civil Engineering Department admitted to a major change of heart regarding its educational philosophy. Ever since its earliest days the department had emphasized how "basic" civil engineering was, and how necessary it was for students to learn the fundamentals of surveying, mechanics, and structural analysis. Traditionally, the department had viewed nontechnical courses as unimportant, noting only in passing that students were expected to take enough nontechnical courses "to provide training for good citizenship."[19] By 1949, though, this philosophy had changed, and the department became almost poetic in its enthusiasm for nontechnical courses. Its new goal was to teach students the working principles on which all civil engineering problems are based. These principles, the department told prospective students,

> are obtained in a study of basic English, mathematics, and forces; together with the chemical, biological and physical changes which take place in order to produce a required result. The satisfaction of human wants at the least cost—the major aim of engineering—implies that the engineer know something of the human relations involved. Therefore the student is given an opportunity to learn something of the story of people as well as of things; to learn some of the effects of his work on the social, political, cultural, and economic aspects of ordinary lives so that good engineers may also be good citizens."[20]

The Electrical Engineering Department agreed with these sentiments. After noting that an exceptional knowledge of mathematics and physical sciences formed the basis for an electrical engineering education, the department noted that "an engineer must live with other people, and, in fact his contacts with the public are frequent. Therefore, a . . . vital part of an engineer's training is in the fields of the social sciences and the humanities [which are] just as essential as the scientific and technological courses."[21]

Although World War II had been a difficult and challenging experience for the School of Engineering, it provided the faculty with insight into what the future of the engineering profession was likely to be. The achievements of engineering in producing nuclear weapons and other advanced armaments were obvious to all. The beginning of the Cold War, with its seemingly endless need to produce sophisticated weapons, made it clear that engineers were likely to play a very important role in the development of the nation's defenses. Federally sponsored research organizations were beginning to achieve prominence in the South, an area which clearly could provide many opportunities for a properly equipped and staffed school of engineering. The federal government was in the process of establishing the Institute for Nuclear Studies at Oak Ridge and the U.S. Army Corps of Engineers was expanding its research facility at Vicksburg. Mississippi State could not hope to seriously participate in organizations such as these, or to engage in other defense-related research, without a school of engineering capable of offering graduate studies and engaging in research.[22]

The main obstacle to the School of Engineering's efforts to achieve a stature high enough to permit it develop a research program and join its peers in helping to develop advanced technologies had long been a lack of money for salaries, equipment, and facilities. Because of its chronic underfunding Mississippi State had developed a reputation as one of several institutions "well-known as having inadequate salary scales."[23] The Gibson Report had noted that Mississippi State ranked second and third from the bottom of the national list of land-grant colleges in terms of salaries paid full and associate professors of engineering. The school was firmly at the bottom of the list of salaries paid instructors and assistant professors. The report had urged the board to upgrade faculty salaries, but nothing had been done. This situation had resulted in a high turnover in the lower ranks; by 1948, it had become all but impossible to employ either assistant or associate professors. During the 1947-48 academic year, for example, thirty-one of fifty faculty members resigned to move to industry or to other colleges and universities with higher salary scales.[24]

Fortunately, the energies unleashed by the war extended to Mississippi, and the postwar years saw a considerable improvement in funding for the college. Between 1948 and 1952 three new buildings of great importance to the School of Engineering were authorized by the legislature. Both the 47,000-square-foot Patterson Engineering Laboratories and the Mitchell Memorial Library were dedicated on October 24, 1950; the Ethridge Chemical Engineering Building was authorized in 1952. While the engineering faculty did not use the library extensively, its construction allowed the school to make new use of space that had housed the engineering library. New leadership also brought new vigor to the college. After receiving a vote of no-confidence from the board of trustees, President Humphrey left Mississippi State for the University of Wyoming and was succeeded by Fred Tom Mitchell, a graduate of Mississippi A & M and a dedicated academic with a doctorate from Cornell. The School of Engineering came under new leadership upon the retirement of Dean Patterson, who had served the college for forty years. "Dean Pat" had served the School of Engineering in several capacities since arriving in 1909. He began his career as an associate professor of electrical engineering, became professor of physics in 1911, and professor of electrical engineering in 1914 which then included responsibility for the campus electrical services. He had been dean of the School of Engineering since 1930.[25]

His successor was Harold von Neufville Flinsch, who had been hired as associate dean a year earlier with the understanding that he would move into the deanship upon Patterson's retirement. Flinsch was the first member of the engineering faculty since Moody to hold a Ph.D. degree. He had earned his degree in civil engineering at the University of Minnesota in 1946, where he had written his doctoral dissertation on the energy contained in ocean waves. Flinsch, who came to Mississippi State from Bucknell University, was an urbane, widely traveled man fluent in German and French and with six years of experience in engineering research. Flinsch's mission was twofold. First, it was clear that the professional qualifications of the faculty had to be upgraded if Mississippi State was to compete with its peers and maintain accreditation. President Mitchell had made employment of a higher percentage of faculty members with terminal degrees one of his main priorities, although the rapid growth in student enrollment after World War II, coupled with a national shortage of holders of the Ph.D. degree and the uncompetitive salaries paid by Mississippi State, made the goal difficult to achieve.[26]

The second part of Flinsch's mission was to expand the research programs of the School of Engineering. He hoped soon to permit faculty members to spend half of their time on research in the Engineering Research Station, where state industries and agencies could find assistance in solving their engineering problems at relatively small cost. He also planned to pursue outside funding for research projects, although the faculty's lack of advanced degrees and research experience made the prospects for such assistance rather dim. Indeed, in 1948, when Flinsch assumed the directorship of the Engineering and Industrial Research Station, the only active research projects underway besides McCain's work on nailed joints were based on Flinsch's own research that he had begun at Minnesota and Bucknell. Holmes, who was contemplating beginning research on the cooling properties of noncylindrical bodies, had obtained a $500 grant from the American Society of Refrigerating Engineers. Because of his heavy teaching and administrative load, he had not advanced beyond the formative stage.[27]

Given the massive teaching loads of the engineering faculty, their general lack of experience in conducting research, and the inadequate facilities, it was unrealistic to expect much research from the regular teaching faculty. A record enrollment of 1020 students, not including agricultural and chemical engineering, placed great pressure on both faculty and facilities. Enrollment had increased some 300 percent since the 1920s when new space had last been available, and before the completion of the Patterson Laboratories, the School of Engineering was spread out over the campus, occupying about two-thirds of the Engineering Building, one-half of the third floor of Lee Hall, and six temporary buildings on the former golf course. Until new space could be assigned to the research station, wrote Patterson in his last annual report, its activity would be limited to reviews of research work completed at other institutions something "necessarily sterile and parasitical in nature."[28] No original research could be expected from the School of Engineering, wrote Flinsch, until policies were adopted that permitted reduced instructional loads and made funds available for research expenses. Holmes's experience illustrates the problems involved in doing research at Mississippi State College at that time. In a questionnaire he filled out just before the end of World War II he responded "none" when asked to list research projects in progress. When asked to outline his planned research program, he wrote: "I plan none. I have started one project which I gave up because of a lack of equipment, skilled help, and money."[29]

Under these circumstances new ideas and new methods were called for if a research program was to become a reality. It was clear that if Mississippi State planned to become a research institution, it would have to do so with little or no new investment in salaries or equipment. The Research Station was so poorly funded, for example, that, in 1948, the only equipment it could acquire was a used press for testing the strength of concrete, a 35-millimeter camera, typewriter, wire recorder, and hand-cranked calculator.[30]

Almost since his arrival at Mississippi State, President Mitchell had been exploring ways in which the college could become involved in research sponsored by the federal government. He saw no reason why Mississippi State should not participate in the defense-related research programs that were being developed throughout the country after World War II. He had become interested in finding ways for the University to participate in the research programs sponsored by the Office of Naval Research (ONR) which began supporting various research projects throughout the United States in the late 1940s.

In 1946, Mitchell asked the college faculty to submit ideas for research projects, which he planned to submit to ONR. The resulting document, astonishing in its breadth, seemed to include a little of everything. The list also illustrated the painful fact that most Mississippi State College faculty members really had no clear idea what scholarly research was. Faculty members gave Mitchell numerous ideas for research projects. Dorothy Dickins of the Department of Food and Nutrition, for instance, thought she might like to study the "food habits and preferences of young men," while Ross E. Hutchins of Entomology proposed studying ways to eradicate snails in ponds and streams. Most of the proposals submitted by the engineering departments came from Electrical Engineering and involved such prosaic ideas as developing ways to predict when vacuum tubes were likely to fail, or studying methods of recharging dry-cell batteries. McCain proposed recycling his TVA project on nailed wood joints.[31]

President Mitchell submitted the list of proposed projects in quadruplicate, and the ONR promptly declined to fund any of them, citing "budgetary limitations and other circumstances," although it did assign projects to institutions in other Southern states, a course of action which President Mitchell indignantly protested. Even Chemistry, which traditionally was the strongest research department at Mississippi State because of its association with the State Chemical Laboratory, was unable to participate in ONR-sponsored research. A Birmingham research institution asked Mississippi

State to join in submitting a cooperative research plan to ONR, and President Mitchell asked Clay Lyle, dean of the School of Science, to respond. Lyle told the Southern Research Institute that he had consulted with W. F. Hand, Vice President of Mississippi State and M. P. Ethridge, State Chemist, who agreed that the college's chemistry laboratories were so overcrowded and "inadequately equipped for advanced research" that there was little reason to pursue the idea further. Given the nature of the faculty and facilities at Mississippi State, attracting federal funding for research seemed all but hopeless.[32]

Flinsch was an aircraft enthusiast who had earned an instrument rating and who regularly flew his own airplane on business and pleasure trips. He was also deeply interested in sailplanes. This combination of interests gave Flinsch an idea for the organization of an entirely new and different research program for Mississippi State. Research projects in aeronautics using sailplanes as data collectors, he thought, could be established at minimal cost which would be unique in the United States. "For over twenty years," mused Flinsch, "I have wondered why other countries have not benefitted to the fullest extent by the German experiences [sic] in sailplane research." The German experience was particularly instructive, he noted, because most of that country's research with sailplanes during the prewar period had been accomplished by scientists in such "impecunious" institutions as the University of Darmstadt and the Aachen Institute of Technology. Flinsch knew that the research had been valuable because many of the high-performance aircraft Germany used during the war had been developed using knowledge gained from sailplane research. If poorly funded institutions such as those in Darmstadt and Aachen could achieve such impressive results in sailplane research, perhaps Mississippi State could do the same thing.[33]

Evidently, Flinsch had been thinking for some time about the possibility of beginning a research program using sailplanes. He soon entered into negotiations with August Raspet, a prominent sailplane specialist, immediately after his appointment as Director of the Research Station in February, 1948. Raspet was a graduate of the Carnegie Institute of Technology and had received his Ph.D. degree in physics from the University of Maryland in 1942. By 1947, he had thirteen inventions in what he called "applied physics" to his credit and had delivered or published twenty papers.[34]

Raspet had participated in several projects where gliders had been used to obtain data on atmospheric turbulence. The most notable of these was the work he did in 1946 as director of research for the glider phase of the Thunderstorm Project, a large-scale federally-sponsored effort to learn more about the forces created during thunderstorms and to study how these forces affected aircraft. Essentially, the project involved combining large amounts of data collected by ground weather stations, balloons, powered planes, and gliders over a 100-square-mile section of central Florida. Raspet's role in the project involved piloting a sailplane into thunderheads, where the glider would be seized by the fierce winds within the clouds. Measurements of the storm's forces could then be made by plotting the sailplane's motions. After the project ended, Raspet became director of research for a firm known as the Aerophysics Institute where he had obtained a research grant from ONR to study airflow patterns over long mountain ridges, using sailplanes as measuring instruments. The purpose of the study was to measure the vertical and horizontal components of the flowing air as well as its temperature and pressure.35

Raspet could not refuse an opportunity to operate his own independent sailplane research program, and he began work at Mississippi State as project leader in February 1949. He was the most productive and experienced research scientist the School of Engineering had ever had, and Flinsch was not sure where to house him. First, as a physicist, Raspet was not qualified to teach in one of the established engineering departments, and he certainly did not want to teach elementary physics. Also, Flinsch had employed Raspet in part because the established faculty simply did not have the time or experience to conduct research programs (as President Mitchell's list of possible activities illustrated). In a way, Flinsch seems to have thought it best to keep Raspet as isolated as possible from the existing departments in order to make it clear to all that he was not a member of the teaching faculty. Thus, when Raspet arrived on campus he moved into his own newly-created department called "Aerophysics." As A. G. Holmes put it, funds were "diverted" from other long-established engineering departments. Although Holmes was not initially enthusiastic about the new department, he later called it a "wise move."36

Raspet had come to Mississippi State largely because he had been promised the complete freedom to do the work he loved the most—use sailplanes to study fundamental aspects of flight. His choice of an introductory research project certainly seemed somewhat bizarre to traditional

Mississippians. Almost immediately, Raspet began using his sailplanes to study the characteristics of bird flight by following buzzards as they soared over the outskirts of Starkville. By observing the birds, he thought, basic knowledge of aeronautics could be obtained which might help improve the performance of slow-moving aircraft. "We will fly and soar with these birds," Raspet said, "observing how they use their feathers in this way to reduce drag and attempt to incorporate a comparable system in our own sailplane, possibly eventually reducing wing span."[37] Raspet knew that the armed forces were interested in this type of research because of their need to develop short-take-off-and-landing (STOL) fixed-wing aircraft that could be used for battlefield liaison. The preliminary research bore fruit, and in 1951, the Aerophysics Department received a $16,000 contract to study the performance of soaring birds. What was to become a long and productive involvement in aeronautical research was launched.[38]

Raspet required minimal equipment for the research projects he envisioned. The Research Station purchased a Stearman biplane to tow the sailplanes aloft, as well as a jeep for ground-towing operations. It refurbished four Lasiter-Kauffman planes and purchased several sailplanes. Shelley Charles of Atlanta presented a high-performance sailplane to the Engineering Research Station for use in meteorological studies. Now that the basic fleet of planes had been prepared, wrote Flinsch, the way was clear for the Aerophysics Department to begin basic research projects in meteorology and aerodynamics that could not be accomplished anyplace else.[39]

Although the war had created a need for engineers, the influx of veterans studying under the G.I. Bill of Rights quickly satisfied the demands of the job market, and by the spring of 1949, employers had dramatically decreased the numbers of new engineers hired. Employers who had once competed with each another to find engineering graduates disappeared from campus. Even the expedient of publishing booklets for potential employers advertising graduates like so many pieces of merchandise failed to stem the downward decline in job openings.[40]

Although the Bureau of Labor Statistics predicted that the decline in employment opportunities would be temporary, and that there would be an increase in employment opportunities beginning in 1953, student interest in engineering education fell precipitously. Engineering students traditionally have been very career-oriented, and reports of unemployed engineers tend to translate quickly into declining enrollments. Indeed, since World War II a major problem in engineering education has been the tendency for enrollments in colleges of engineering to follow a pattern of steep increases and declines, depending on how stable engineering employment was at a particular moment. Much of this enrollment instability has been caused by the extensive involvement of the federal government in generating employment opportunities for engineers through military or aerospace programs. Flush times with many job offers and high salaries have been followed by recessions typified by the proverbial engineer driving a taxicab. This unpredictable cycle has been confusing for engineering educators and students alike, as it does not follow the usual business cycle. Engineers dependent on specialized defense-related programs often have found their profession depressed while the rest of the economy prospers.

The postwar period provided the first experience with defense-related enrollment changes, and the enrollment in the School of Engineering dropped dramatically. From a high of 975 students in the fall of 1947, enrollment dropped to 500 in the spring of 1950 and 350 in 1951. Although Dean Flinsch thought this might provide an opportunity to reduce teaching loads to a level that would provide adequate preparation time and opportunities for faculty members to provide individual instruction, he was overly optimistic. The state forced budget cuts which, coupled with leaves of absence, forced Flinsch to reduce the teaching staff from 55 in 1950 to close to 40 in 1951.[41]

While a variety of explanations for the decline in enrollment could be advanced, the Mississippi State engineering faculty seemed to believe that the courses required for graduation were inadequate in number and not sufficiently technical, and between 1950 and 1953 another major revision of the curriculum was phased in. The liberal-arts component of the curriculum decreased and the total number of semester hours required for graduation gradually increased to 152 by 1953, which meant that students had to complete an average of nineteen hours per semester. Twelve hours of electives were added, which were intended mainly to provide greater variety in fields of technical interest.[42] The only courses in the humanities and social sciences to survive were American Government, World Civilization, and American Civilization; all of the rest were replaced with technical courses. In practice, this meant that after the end of the first sophomore semester, engineering students received no exposure to nontechnical offerings. Certainly, the lists of electives provided little relief. All engineering students taking advanced ROTC had no electives. Aeronautical Engineering students were advised to choose their elective courses from a list of five: Electronics, Business Correspondence, Speech, Vector Analysis, and Modern Physics. The same situation obtained in the other engineering departments. Although Civil Engineering and Electrical Engineering retained their catalog introductions, which stressed the need for their students to take courses that would enable them to develop a certain level of social and political understanding, the actual courses required of students showed that this philosophy had largely been abandoned. Electrical and Mechanical Engineering listed the two previously required humanities courses in their lists of electives; but, given the highly technical traditions of the school, it is doubtful if many advisors recommended these courses to students. The curriculum was broadened somewhat in 1953 by reintroducing the concept of required nontechnical elective courses. Mechanical Engineering led the way by requiring six such courses, Electrical Engineering required two, Civil Engineering required three, and Aeronautical Engineering four. Agricultural Engineering required none.43

Nevertheless, as the seventy-fifth anniversary of education in the mechanic arts at Mississippi State approached, the school had begun to tread a path that eventually led to marked improvements in educational quality. An accreditation team from the ECPD visited campus in 1952 and granted accreditation to all of the engineering programs except Chemical and Agricultural Engineering. Agricultural Engineering received accreditation in 1954. Although only electrical engineering received the full five-year accreditation, the rest were accredited for either two or three years, and optimists in the school hoped for eventual full accreditation of all the departments. Enrollment had increased enormously from its postwar lows. By 1956, the School of Engineering was the largest of the schools, enrolling 1100 students which accounted for about one-third of Mississippi State's students. By 1957, it had enrolled as many students as the next two largest schools, Business and Agriculture, put together. It even began to teach a handful of women students eager to find a niche in the male-dominated engineering profession.44

Although the teaching loads had become so high as to bring nearly all faculty research to a standstill, the work of August Raspet and the Aerophysics Department was sufficient to bring national recognition as a research institution to Mississippi State for the first time. With the assistance of ONR, Raspet and his team began to study the behavior of air flowing over an airfoil at low speeds. This research, which grew out of their studies of soaring birds, was enough to gain the Mississippi State College Engineering and Industrial Research Station active membership in the Engineering College Research Council of the American Society for Engineering Education, an organization that had earlier chosen Flinsch as its president.[45]

Thus, by 1957, the School of Engineering at Mississippi State was better than it ever had been before. More members of the faculty had earned advanced degrees, the curriculum was more sophisticated, and the faculty was becoming more aware of the value of research. Major efforts by Harold Flinsch and H. P. Neal had resulted in improved relations with Mississippi manufacturers who finally were beginning to appreciate the contributions that the School of Engineering could make to their industries.[46]

The main obstacle in the road to quality engineering education, of course, was funding which had not in any way kept up with the increased enrollment since World War II. Even this seemingly intractable obstacle was about to be pushed aside. Throughout its history the School of Engineering had found that most of its major moves toward improvement had not been the result of self-study but had come about through the impact of outside forces. When the students arrived on campus in September 1957, the faculty of the School of Engineering was prepared to offer them the usual courses of instruction, and the administration was probably prepared to make the usual complaints about lack of resources and professional development. Yet, the School was about to be shocked into motion again by outside forces in a way that none of the members of the faculty or of the administration could ever have imagined when the academic year began.

CHAPTER SIX

The Research University

On October 4, 1957 the Soviet Union launched *Sputnik I*, the first manmade satellite to orbit the earth. On November 3, the Soviets sent the much larger *Sputnik II* into space carrying a dog. These two events shocked the United States into a frenzy of self-examination. Although the Cold War between the United States and the Soviet Union had been underway since the end of post-World War II Allied cooperation, and fear of Soviet nuclear attack was in some ways justified, Americans remained confident that the technological prowess that had produced the atomic and hydrogen bombs would deter potential enemies into the indefinite future. The faint beeps sent back to earth by *Sputnik I* blasted these assumptions and told Americans in unmistakable terms that their happy assumption of indefinite technological superiority was false.[1]

World War II, of course, was a major turning point in the history of the United States and the world. It caused the combatants on both sides to concentrate their national political, economic, and intellectual resources in a way never before seen. The United States, Great Britain, Germany, Japan, and the Soviet Union mobilized the energies of their scientists to explore new scientific theories for their potential application to the war effort. Four technological breakthroughs emerged from this massive concentration of scientific and intellectual talent: the atomic bomb and electronic computer (developed in the United States), the ballistic missile (first produced in Germany), and radar (invented in Great Britain). This technology has so altered the world of the twentieth century that it is practically impossible to escape its influence. These achievements all have one thing in common: Unlike previous revolutionizing technologies—such as the steam engine or the airplane, which were largely the creations of individual inventors—the new technologies emerged from national commitments to massive research-and-development operations.[2]

Certainly *Sputnik I* and *II* emerged from this new national commitment. The militarized Soviet political and economic system, which had already produced atomic and hydrogen bombs, won the first round of the space race by concentrating enormous resources on a clearly defined goal. The Soviet system, traditionally so abhorrent to Americans, had rapidly developed the means to threaten the United States with mass destruction. The same type of missiles that had launched the Soviet satellites could surely deliver nuclear bombs to the North American continent.

The lesson of the Soviet challenge seemed clear to American leaders who wished to build on the national initiatives in research and development that had emerged from World War II. They argued that the liberal, individualistic, almost anarchic methods that had long governed technological innovation in the United States had clearly become inadequate. Cries for a national restructuring of scientific and technological talent sufficient to match or even overwhelm the Soviets came from all quarters. The powers of the federal government, went the argument, must be concentrated to achieve a level of scientific and technological excellence that would guarantee American national security and prove the superiority of the nation's institutions. The Manhattan Project was the model on which all future national endeavors should be based.[3]

President Dwight D. Eisenhower was very dubious about such arguments. He feared the political, social and economic consequences of restructuring American institutions along the lines of the Manhattan Project. This is what Eisenhower meant when he referred to the dangers of creating a "military-industrial complex." The young President John F. Kennedy and his advisors, on the other hand, were much more willing to use the resources of the federal government to bring about change. When Kennedy spoke of a "New Frontier" in his 1961 inaugural address, he was welcoming a world where highly structured research organizations, developed under the aegis of the federal government, would attack all problems. Kennedy's ringing challenge was more persuasive than Eisenhower's sober warning, and soon the United States had plunged headlong into a future where dozens of Manhattan Project-style initiatives would touch the lives of all Americans.[4]

In spite of reassurances from cautious leaders such as Eisenhower, the people of the United States soon perceived the launching of the Soviet space satellites as a direct threat to the nation's survival. This view was not unreasonable, considering the high level of technological sophistication required to place *Sputnik II* into orbit. The satellite remained attached to its final rocket stage, and together the two parts weighed almost six tons. Thus, the national hysteria produced by Soviet achievements in space generated enormous political pressure throughout late 1957 and 1958 for a crash program to counteract the perceived Soviet superiority in research and development. The highly charged political atmosphere was dramatized by a series of hearings held by Senator Lyndon B. Johnson early in 1958. He wanted to publicize what he considered a perilous and desperate situation requiring massive federal involvement in the nation's educational system. "Defense," Johnson wrote, "involves the total effort of a nation. . . . There can be no adequate defense for the U.S. except in a reservoir of trained and educated minds. . . .[5]

It soon became clear that a major transformation of American attitudes toward higher education and its relationship with the government was underway. Throughout American history the federal government had asked institutions of higher learning to become involved in meeting specific educational goals only during the two world wars, and then only to provide rather limited kinds of specialized training. Now, however, colleges and universities found themselves major players in the race to out-educate and out-engineer the Soviet Union. Suddenly, Mississippi State and its School of Engineering were on the front lines of the Cold War.

Unfortunately, Mississippi State was poorly positioned to participate in a national effort to defeat the Soviet Union through superior education. Years of low salaries, all-consuming teaching duties, and little or no money for travel to professional meetings had isolated the engineering faculty in a way that few of them fathomed. Since many of the most significant developments in engineering during and after World War II had been classified and therefore were not publishable, few faculty members outside the Aerophysics Department knew much about the new technologies of satellites, rockets, and computers. "The impetus provided by World War II, the Korean conflict and the so-called cold war to scientific development leading up to Sputinc I [sic]," wrote A. G. Holmes, "was almost unknown to us." The engineering faculty had been "lulled into believing that in training our students in the conventional manner we were accomplishing our appointed task. We were ripe for a rude and shocking awakening." Quality engineering education, Holmes concluded, came "not from old books . . . but from new knowledge, from men working to develop new things using new concepts."[6]

As was often the case throughout its history, Mississippi State was suffering from a serious lack of funding which, in the case of the School of Engineering, threatened to bring into question its all-important ECPD accreditation. Although the School of Engineering had made significant strides toward improved quality during the postwar period, the standards of the engineering profession were advancing faster, and the pressures created by the hysteria of 1957 and 1958 only served to accelerate the trend. In 1954, for example, the ECPD conducted one of its regular inspections of the engineering program: its conclusions did not make pleasant reading. The Department of Electrical Engineering, which had become the strongest department in the School, received accreditation for only three years. The evaluators were struck by the low level of support funds and salaries, particularly at the rank of associate and full professor. The criticisms of the ECPD evaluators were completely justified, wrote Harry Simrall, head of the Department of Electrical Engineering. Graduating seniors were receiving higher starting salaries in entry-level positions than were the highest-paid members of the faculty, some of whom had twenty years' experience and who were "beginning to lose hope of the situation ever being any better." Because of inadequate funds with which to employ faculty members, the Department was using undergraduates to teach laboratory sections. "Using students to teach students," Simrall concluded dryly, "is certainly not to be desired." He finished by begging Dean Flinsch to do something "to give this department a spark of hope and encouragement in its efforts to do an acceptable job of teaching and research."[7]

Even though these criticisms were serious, they could be addressed in a straightforward way by improving salaries and equipment and by decreasing teaching loads. Mississippi State made a valiant attempt to meet the criticisms of the 1954 ECPD evaluators and was able to persuade the association to forego the interim inspection that had been scheduled for 1957 by raising salaries and eliminating the undergraduate laboratory instructors. Yet, the school soon found that it was shooting at a moving target. What Simrall called the "astounding engineering and scientific developments of recent years" made the relatively simple suggestions for improvement proposed by the evaluators in 1954 seem almost quaint. By 1959, the ECPD not only demanded improved salaries and working conditions, but was also insisting on wholesale revisions in curricula and a greater emphasis on research.[8]

Thus, in preparation for the next full-scale ECPD evaluation, the School of Engineering again undertook a redesign of its curriculum. Simrall knew that the almost purely technical curriculum established in the wake of the postwar enrollment declines was rapidly becoming outmoded. In light of the postwar need for more and better engineers the American Society for Engineering Education commissioned another report on engineering curricula to examine once again the perennial question of whether engineering educators should provide students with a professional or a liberal education. L. E. Grinter directed the study which proposed revisions of the engineering curriculum so as to base it on the "engineering sciences" defined as the study of basic scientific principles as related to engineering problems and situations. The study recommended that engineering schools base their engineering science courses on two areas of study: the "mechanical phenomena of solids, liquids, and gases," and electrical phenomena. Naturally, such education required a serious grounding in mathematics, chemistry, and physics. The report also acknowledged complaints received from industry which "placed great emphasis on the inability of engineers to express themselves in clear, concise, effective, and interesting language." Thus, it asked engineering educators to recognize that the humanities should be treated as integral parts of one total curriculum. Although Grinter's report was published before the launching of *Sputnik I*, its recommendations for a liberal, science-based engineering curriculum were only reinforced by the beginning of the space age.[9]

Harry Simrall became dean of the school in 1957 when Harold Flinsch departed for the University of South Carolina. Simrall had been associated with Mississippi State since his arrival as a freshman in 1930, and had served the college continuously with the exception of a year of graduate work at the University of Illinois and a year working for Westinghouse during World War II. Although Simrall's teaching and administrative experience had all been at Mississippi State, he remained abreast of national trends in engineering education and wanted to build on Flinsch's efforts to make Mississippi State competitive with its peer institutions.[10]

Simrall welcomed the revisions in the engineering curriculum that the ASEE had developed. He knew that many members of the engineering faculty members viewed the revisions with suspicion because they placed little emphasis on the development of skills and how-to-do courses such as shops, drawing, and surveying, replacing this training with basic physical sciences and mathematics and the engineering sciences. These faculty members did not accept the argument that even though the resulting engineering graduate was less skilled at drawing, shop practices, and surveying, it was better for the graduate to think in terms of theoretical analysis and design and leave the "practical" engineering skills to craftsmen and technicians. Yet, it must always be remembered, Simrall told a group of engineering educators assembled at the University of Alabama that they were responsible for training people who must be capable of dealing with problems that were fifteen or twenty years into the future, and which were at present "unknown and undreamed of." Some faculty members worried that new curricula might be dangerous in the long run. Holmes feared that the undergraduate program had been forced into "a pattern so scientific" that it was almost undistinguishable from a school of science. He even feared for the continued existence of undergraduate schools of engineering on the grounds that few universities would be willing to support what were essentially two schools of science. Nevertheless, Holmes welcomed the liberalized curriculum because he believed that the traditional narrow training received by engineering students meant that "those who remain in engineering practice were educated to be exploited" because they lacked the general education necessary to move easily from one area to another.[11]

If the school wished to retain its accreditation it had little choice in the matter. Upon Simrall's recommendation, the engineering faculty agreed to undertake a massive restructuring of the curriculum. The faculty reduced the number of hours required for graduation to 140 and established stiffer admission requirements for prospective students who also had to demonstrate greater proficiency in mathematics. The Engineering School stopped accepting credit earned through participation in Advanced ROTC. The most important change was the reorganization of the curriculum into four integrated stems. They were physical science and mathematics, humanities and social studies, engineering science, and engineering analysis and design.

Each sequence was divided into smaller units. The sequence in engineering science, for example, consisted of studies in the mechanics of solids, fluid mechanics, thermodynamics, transfer and rate mechanisms, electrical theory, and the nature and properties of materials. The engineering analysis and design sequence involved studying the creative and practical phases of economic design, involving analysis, synthesis, and engineering research and development. This sequence, the School of Engineering told its students, was the most distinctive feature of the engineering curricula, since it provided "the element of creative design which distinguishes the engineer from the pure scientist."[12]

The new program resulted in the addition of numerous courses in the humanities and social sciences. Aeronautical and Mechanical engineering students, for example, took U.S. History, American Government, World Civilization, European Literature, United States Literature, and two electives in the humanities. Agricultural Engineering, which had resisted past attempts to install required nontechnical courses, now required all of the above except for World Civilization and one fewer humanities elective. Civil Engineering adopted the same curriculum as Aeronautical Engineering, although students were allowed to choose between the humanities and the social sciences when selecting electives.[13]

Thus, when the inspection team from the ECPD visited the campus in 1959, it found that the School of Engineering had made great strides in its efforts to improve. The rapid development of the various branches of engineering had outpaced it, however. Electrical Engineering had improved sufficiently to receive the full five-year accreditation, whereas all of the other departments were accredited for two or three years. The inspection team found that although salaries had improved somewhat, they were still low even for schools in the South. Also, teaching loads were far too high, turnover was too great, and not enough faculty members held degrees from institutions other than Mississippi State. With such high teaching loads, the ECPD investigating committee noted, "a professor has little time and energy to maintain an adequate knowledge of a fast-moving field, such as engineering and the sciences." The report went on to criticize the lack of research by faculty members. Despite the 1958 reforms, the ECPD complained about inadequate mathematics and science requirements, and a system that allowed students to graduate without demonstrating adequate ability in fundamental science and engineering courses.[14]

Although reforms in the engineering curriculum made in the wake of *Sputnik* have remained essentially intact, Mississippi State proponents of practical engineering education were given an opportunity to demonstrate the value of the how-to-do-it approach in the mid-1960s. On January 21, 1964, Paul B. Johnson, Jr., the newly elected governor of Mississippi, delivered an inaugural address that encouraged those interested in practical engineering education. Whereas his immediate predecessors, James P. Coleman and Ross Barnett, had devoted little of their inaugural addresses to education, except to defend racially segregated schools, Johnson did not mention segregation in his address, and instead made the cornerstone of his program a plan to concentrate the educational resources of the state on economic development. He promised not to conduct "a rear-guard defense of yesterday," but to undertake an "all out assault for our share of tomorrow." Part of Governor Johnson's plan involved a major initiative in technological education to "custom-train" workers to be employed in the new industries that would be attracted to Mississippi.[15]

Johnson appointed a committee to establish a program within the state's existing institutions to train engineering and scientific technicians. The result was the Mississippi Technical Institute Act of 1964, which authorized the board of trustees to develop technical institutes that would complement the existing programs in the junior and senior colleges. The board of trustees gave the College of Engineering at Mississippi State administrative responsibility for the new program based in Gulfport at an abandoned Navy base. The four-year Engineering Technology Program was supposed to provide students with an education that would enable them to apply technical knowledge to the solution of industrial problems. Initially students could follow curricula in construction and electronic engineering technology. Later, with the assistance of the Sea Grant Consortium, the college added a curriculum in marine engineering technology.[16]

The engineering technology program, however, was either an idea whose time had not yet come, or an idea whose time had come and gone. The facilities at the old naval base were far from adequate; the state did not provide sufficient funding for the program; and residents of the Gulf Coast could not themselves provide improved facilities. Although graduates received high beginning salaries, the program attracted few students; and outside evaluators viewed it as an unnecessary drain on resources. Others feared that if it were allowed to remain on the coast the institute might one day generate enough political support so that the legislature would be persuaded to make it a free-standing four-year college. Therefore, in 1969, the board of trustees moved the program from Gulfport to the main campus, where it languished until it finally died in 1984. Politicians from the Gulf Coast cried foul, viewing the move as retaliation by north Mississippi for the Gulf Coast's torpedoing of a highway-construction program that would primarily have helped the northern part of the state.[17]

One reason why Mississippi State had offered as much of a how-to curriculum as it had during the post-war years, and why many faculty members resisted science-based engineering education, was because the school relied so heavily on recent graduates without advanced degrees to do much of the teaching. Thus, when the ECPD team inspected the Mechanical Engineering Department in 1959 the members told Holmes in no uncertain terms that the department would have to employ more faculty members with Ph.D. degrees if it wished to be reaccredited in 1964. Holmes knew that whereas curriculum changes could be made by simply changing course names, if the school used that tactic without "radically and comprehensively changing the content . . . we would be attempting a fraud." It was essential, Holmes wrote, to develop a faculty with greater competence in the engineering sciences and in the effective use of mathematics. He also thought that the faculty needed to be more invloved in research. Holmes realized that the existing faculty would not see the new order as a pleasant prospect. The changes in curriculum that were contemplated, and the anticipated increase in the number of students, he wrote, would require psychological adjustments as well as organizational changes that few even wished to think about.[18]

The question was how to obtain such faculty members? There were two options. One was to provide enough graduate work within the School of Engineering so that recent graduates could obtain Ph.D. degrees while serving as teaching assistants. The other was to employ faculty members with Ph.D. degrees granted elsewhere. The first method was nearly impossible at Mississippi State, since so few faculty members were qualified to offer instruction at the doctoral level. The second was equally difficult because the School of Engineering would not be allowed to pay salaries sufficient to attract qualified faculty members, making the "probability of our obtaining a satisfactory man with a Ph.D almost zero."[19]

Holmes had been following the first policy for years before accreditation had come to depend on employing faculty members with Ph.D. degrees. He had routinely offered recent graduates teaching positions with the understanding that they work toward a master's degree. He hoped that as these graduates acquired the master's degree and left, graduates from other universities would materialize. Unfortunately, such faculty members rarely appeared. Nevertheless, the system worked until the ECPD began insisting that engineering students possess greater mathematical sophistication and requiring that engineering courses be placed on a scientific basis.

Holmes found a solution midway betwen the two options. Several able students who had graduated recently expressed interest in pursuing the Ph.D. degree, and Holmes promised them faculty positions if they would obtain a Ph.D. Meanwhile, the Ford Foundation had instituted a program of grants to assist engineering graduates who wished to earn a doctorate and Holmes offered these graduates informal leaves of absence, which he thought more binding than formal leaves of absence, probably because they were moral, rather than legal, obligations. Holmes "held [them] with light strings which were twitched occasionally to remind them of us." Holmes's plan worked. His list of the men employed under this system contains the names of a number of faculty members who have been instrumental in making Mississippi State a nationally recognized institution.[20]

Simrall knew that the modest salary increases that had been implemented, and the changes in curricula that the faculty had approved, would not completely satisfy the ECPD and warned President Ben Hilbun, who had succeeded the deceased Mitchell in 1954, that he should expect a short accreditation because of the "instability of the staff." Building a well-trained faculty with advanced degrees and industrial experience would not be an easy task. Although new positions in the upper ranks had been created, the salaries offered were not competitive nationally and were even well below those paid by nearby institutions. It was clear that with engineering becoming more scientific and specialized, Mississippi State would have to provide higher salaries, decrease teaching loads to a maximum of nine hours per semester, and offer better opportunities for research. Simrall was correct both in expecting minimal accreditation and anticipating the ECPD's reasons. The ECPD granted only minimal accreditation of two or three years to all the departments with the exceptions of Electrical Engineering, which received a five year accreditation, and Chemical Engineering, which was not accredited at all. Although as a result of a progress report, the departments receiving short accreditation later gained interim accreditation until the regularly scheduled inspection in 1964, the school was warned that the ECPD expected it to make significant improvements in reducing teaching loads, improving the curriculum, and professionalizing its design courses.[21]

Not only the School of Engineering, but the entire institution found itself challenged by the great changes in educational standards and expectations that had emerged in the wake of *Sputnik*. "We must keep more jumps ahead of the accreditation hounds than we are at present," wrote John K. Bettersworth, the new vice president for Academic Affairs, in 1962. In large part, Mississippi State's problems with the accrediting agencies stemmed from a confused vision of its place in American higher education. In 1958, the legislature recognized that the school had changed significantly by renaming it Mississippi State University; but this recognition did not mean that those responsible for proposing and approving the name change understood the implications of the statement they were making. By its very nature, a university is a place where scholarship, research, and advanced study can flourish. Leaders of the newly named university and the agencies responsible for guiding it seemed to have difficulty grasping the idea that elevating the institution from its college status involved anything more than a simple name change. It meant that Mississippi State would be expected to assume new responsibilities for research and graduate study while maintaining excellence in undergraduate education. Becoming a university, therefore, required a major adjustment in perception on the part of all concerned with Mississippi State.[22]

Perhaps the most visible symbol of Mississippi State's uncertain status as a university was its president, Benjamin F. Hilbun. Born in a Mississippi town called Cracker's Neck, Hilbun had never earned an advanced degree, nor had he ever been associated with an institution of higher education other than Mississippi State except for a few months at the University of Mississippi before World War I. In fact, he had spent his entire working life in Starkville, working for Mississippi State as its publicity director, registrar, and assistant to President Mitchell. Although he was popular in many quarters, and presided over such major accomplishments as the creation of the College of Arts and Sciences in 1956 and the establishment of doctoral programs in a variety of disciplines, his limited academic experience made it difficult for him to provide the leadership necessary for an institution devoted to research and scholarship as well as undergraduate teaching.[23]

The only unit of the University that had earned any national recognition for research was the Aerophysics Department, headed by August Raspet. The department did not teach undergraduates, although the researchers associated with it gave seminars and supervised graduate theses. As we have seen, President Mitchell had vigorously supported the aerophysics research program, hoping that it would win Mississippi State regional and national recognition. The Aerophysics Department had responded, and it quickly developed an active program of research and publication which led to the winning of lucrative and prestigious contracts. Mitchell was a frail man, however, and by 1952 was in failing health. When he was hospitalized in New Orleans in 1952, most of his administrative duties fell to Hilbun who had become his administrative assistant in 1949. Hilbun became acting president a few months later and was elevated to the presidency in July 1954.

Hilbun did not share Mitchell's interest in promoting research at Mississippi State. His most dramatic statement in that regard was a massive cut in the Aerophysics Department's budget. Institutional funding for the research program was slashed from $32,000 in 1951 to $2,300 in 1952. Funding had been increased only to $3,400 when Hilbun retired in 1960, even though the department had obtained nearly two million dollars in outside support. Whereas, under Mitchell, the College had paid Raspet's salary and that of several of his associates and assistants, the Hilbun budgets provided for only one-third of Raspet's salary. Indeed, when Hilbun was elevated to acting president in 1953, Raspet realized that the only way he could accomplish his objectives was to generate outside political support, a practice almost unheard of outside the School of Agriculture. An example of his efforts was a resolution passed by the Mississippi Aeronautics Commission urging President Hilbun not to harm the Aerophysics Department. The Aeronautics Commission passed a resolution asking the "State of Mississippi, through its Board of Trustees of Institutions of Higher Learning and through its Governor [to] continue the support and foster the further development of the Aerophysics Department." "We are extremely anxious," wrote the commission's Director, C. A. Moore, "that nothing will be forthcoming to cause curtailment of this program that would result in Mississippi losing the leadership that has been gained in this field." Because of the unfavorable research climate during the Hilbun years, Raspet and other faculty members interested in research sometimes seemed to think that they were under assault. In the mid-1950s, for example, Bill Lear, an innovative developer of general aviation aircraft, asked Raspet to study the aerodynamics of the *Lodestar,* one of his best-selling airplanes. He was so happy with the results that he offered to award a large scholarship to Mississippi State for use in the Aerophysics departmental research program. Hilbun refused to accept it. In desperation Raspet told Hilbun in 1956 that the lack of response to his pleas for increased funding had forced him to develop proposals for the establishment of an Aerophysics Institute which he would then move to whatever college or university offered him the best facilities.[24]

It is perhaps unfair to blame Hilbun for having a negative attitude toward scholarly research since the board of trustees and the Mississippi legislature also lacked an understanding of the nature of academic research and were even prepared to use success in research against the institution. In 1954, for example, Dean Flinsch asked Herbert Drennon, dean of the Graduate School, not to publicize in any way the amounts of the contracts Aerophysics had received from ONR. Whereas most institutions would have been proud of such accomplishments, in Mississippi they were best kept hidden so that they could not "be used against us in our struggle for financial survival. . . . If the last two ONR appropriations to Mississippi State College were used against us by unfriendly agents," Flinsch wrote, "we could suffer damage exceeding the . . . cut in the Aerophysics Department last May." The "unfriendly agents" that Flinsch referred to were the board of trustees and legislative supporters of the University of Mississippi who wanted to decrease state appropriations to Mississippi State by amounts corresponding to funds received from nonstate sources. They had already made similar efforts when news of previous appropriations for agricultural research were announced. "In other words," wrote Flinsch, "'Timeo Danaos dona ferentes,' or This is a heck of a time to release information on research appropriation received during the present biennium."[25]

As Holmes pointed out in his critical evaluation of Mechanical Engineering in 1960, Mississippi State faculty members had become isolated during the post-war period and, with the exception of Aerophysics, they were not totally aware of the changes taking place in the research world. An example was Mississippi State's first in-depth self-study for the Southern Association's decennial reaccreditation visit in 1960. "We have looked into our dusty attic and dank cellar, opened closet doors upon our skeletons," wrote the editorial committee. The committee's analysis of individual research produced some surprising results. Outside of the School of Agriculture where faculty members mainly published Mississippi Agricultural Experiment Station Bulletins, the most vigorous research programs were in the School of Arts and Sciences, particularly in the departments of History and Sociology. The School of Engineering provided a weak summation of its research program when it stated "Production of papers for so-called learned journals has been low here, as compared with the larger schools. Lack of time for research and lack of money explain this low production. Certainly there is material in the files of our instructors which should be published."[26]

Whether the regular engineering faculty members had publishable materials in their files or not, little of it saw the light of day, and most scholarly work continued to come from the Aerophysics Department. Although August Raspet and his colleagues maintained their interest in sailplanes as a research platform, the research direction of the Aerophysics Department had become concentrated on studying the principles involved in viscous fluid mechanics. The practical appeal of this research lay in its application to the development of short-take-off-and-landing (STOL) airplanes, which, in the days before fast, reliable helicopters, were of great interest to the armed forces for use in battlefield liaison. The Aerophysics Department had received almost two million dollars from the Office of Naval Research and the U.S. Army Transportation Research Command to support its projects.[27]

The key concepts in the Raspet group's research program involved sophisticated studies of the boundary layer, a thin layer of air that forms over the surface of an aircraft in motion. When this layer is smooth, or laminar, drag on the body in motion is lessened. When the flow of air becomes turbulent, drag increases and lift decreases. Thus, one key to increased efficiency and enhanced performance is maintaining a smooth boundary layer. Raspet's group concentrated on research designed to improve the capabilities of aircraft by maintaining a laminar boundary layer. The first approach involved what Raspet called "geometric boundary layer control." In essence he carefully examined the exterior of aircraft in order to find any irregularity that might cause the airflow to become turbulent. Such factors as poorly fitting access doors, irregularly installed lights and vents, and protruding rivets were viewed as interfering with a laminar boundary layer. The Raspet team modified aircraft so as to eliminate or smooth any part that might cause the boundary layer to become turbulent. In the mid-1950s Raspet had used these techniques to modify a Beech Twin Bonanza supplied by the U.S. Army. The smoothing operations resulted in a 20 percent decrease in power requirements, a corresponding increase in range, and a 14 percent decrease in drag. The Army Transportation Corps was so impressed that it considered modifying its entire fleet so as to incorporate Raspet's suggested changes.[28]

In 1951, Raspet made a discovery that was to shape the research program of the Aerophysics Department and provide it with its first national recognition for engineering research. This discovery, which emerged from the Aerophysics Department's basic research with sailplanes, involved controlling the boundary layer through suction. While Raspet's geometric boundary layer control could be dismissed by critics as little more than the application of well-known aerodynamic principles, his new methodology was unique and innovative. The idea of modifying the boundary layer through suction was not exactly new; previous experimenters had tried to alter it by moving air through slots or large holes. Raspet's research initiative began when he and his colleagues pricked thousands of tiny holes in the wings of one of their sailplanes and installed a battery-powered blower to create an area of lowered air pressure inside the wing. The results were dramatic almost from the beginning. The suction through the holes modified the flow of air over the wings and made the boundary layer almost perfectly laminar. Raspet immediately realized that he had discovered a technique with great potential. "Imagine what an influence our work would have on airship design," he told Bruce Carmichael, an old friend and fellow sailplane enthusiast. "Merely tatoo the fabric and cut the drag," he said. "I think we have a gold mine in the sailplane for viscous flow studies."[29]

Raspet was correct in his assessment of the potential of combining geometric and suction boundary layer control. Both the Army and Navy began contracting with him to perform basic aerodynamic research on light aircraft. They were interested in developing STOL liaison aircraft that could land and take off under adverse battlefield conditions. Basically, Raspet's work for the services involved modifying commercial light aircraft, such as Pipers and Cessnas, to give them STOL capabilities. This research, of course, had applications for the civilian aircraft industry as well.[30]

The result of the Raspet group's research program was a great outpouring of technical papers and graduate theses. By 1960, thirteen graduate students studying under Raspet and other faculty members associated with him had written master's theses on aspects of viscous flow, and researchers associated with Raspet's group had published seventy-four technical papers on sailplanes, fluid flow, and control of the boundary layer. Among these researchers are a number of men who later became members of the Mississippi State University faculty and who were instrumental in developing mechanical and aeronautical research programs at Mississippi State. For example, Joseph J. Cornish, wrote a master's thesis entitled "The Viscous Flow in a Corner Parallel to the Flow" and later published numerous research papers on controlling the boundary layer. He later earned a Ph.D. degree under Raspet. As a graduate assistant David L. Murphree prepared a research note on "Measurements on a Highly Cambered Model Airfoil Section and Experimental Techniques." Donald W. Boatwright, Charles B. Cliett, Graham W. Wells, and Glenn D. Bryant all published papers on boundary layer control while working with Raspet.[31]

In April 1960, Lowell L. Meyer, an employee of the Chance-Vaught Aircraft Company, came to Starkville to learn more about enhancing the performance of light aircraft. Raspet, who liked nothing better than demonstrating the progress of his research, personally took him for a demonstration ride in a Piper Super Cub that had been modified by the Aerophysics group under a contract with the U.S. Army. The plane had received a full-scale geometric and suction boundary layer control treatment. Those who had seen it in the air over Starkville told reporters that the plane "sometimes [traveled] so slow that it appeared to be standing still in midair." In all likelihood, Meyer wanted to see how slowly the Cub could fly without stalling, and Raspet must have been eager to show him. But, something went wrong and the plane crashed, killing Raspet and Meyer.[32]

"To the aerophysics department at State," wrote John Bettersworth, "he was the hope of a wonderful future, a man who carried in his slim carriage the expansion and growth of a whole new world." Raspet's fondest dream was the establishment of an aeronautics institute where basic and applied research could be done with minimal interference. By 1957, Raspet had abandoned his plan to obtain funding for his institute from other states and had developed a detailed proposal for a $500,000 Aerophysics Institute to be built at Mississippi State, which would be funded entirely by the federal government through reimbursement of indirect costs. Although he did not reject Raspet's proposal out of hand, President Hilbun was cool to the idea and refused to give it his support until he could be certain that the institute would receive enough outside funds to support it almost completely. Ultimately Hilbun decided against building the institute at the Starkville airport, offering only space in the new Walker Engineering Laboratories for the Aerophysics research program, an offer Raspet found unacceptable. Raspet had made many friends throughout the state, through his tireless efforts to promote aeronautics, and he kept trying to obtain funds for the research institute with or without Hilbun's support. In 1958 the legislature had passed a concurrent resolution commending Raspet and the Aerophysics Department for their contributions to enhancing the prestige of Mississippi State, and Raspet and Dean Simrall continued to lobby the legislature for a direct appropriation for the Aerophysics Institute. Indeed, Simrall was in Jackson lobbying for the institute when he learned of Raspet's death. The tragedy shocked the legislature into action and it promptly appropriated $500,000 to build the facility. Although Raspet was gone, his memory lives on in the form of the Flight Research Laboratory built at the Starkville Airport, which now bears his name. Completed in the summer of 1962, the laboratory contains 26,400 square feet of hangar floor space as well as fully equipped wood, sheet metal and composite material shops, an instrumentation laboratory, and a control tower. It is one of the best university aeronautical research facilities in the United States and is a tribute to Raspet's energy and perseverance.33

The main project to emerge from the Aerophysics Department after Raspet's death was an aircraft based on the visionary techniques Raspet had developed. Raspet had long believed that an airplane with full STOL characteristics achieved through geometric and suction boundary layer control could be built which also could achieve a fairly fast cruising speed. Such an airplane would both meet military needs for a liaison aircraft and become a "family airplane" in the civilian market. In 1959, the Army signed contracts with Mississippi State to produce a STOL aircraft that was to have a cruising speed of 350 miles per hour but that would be able to land at thirty-five miles per hour. The military officially called the plane the XVIIA, but it was dubbed the MARVEL for "Mississippi Aerophysics Vehicle with Extended Latitude" by Joseph Cornish, Raspet's successor as head of the Aerophysics Department. The aircraft was designed to be built of glass fiber reinforced-polyester to provide a clean surface, and have suction boundary layer control over its wings and some of the fuselage. Power would come from a turboprop engine connected to a ducted pusher propeller located inside a shroud.34

The MARVEL posed many more technological and administrative problems than Raspet had anticipated. The composite materials used to build the fuselage and wings proved to be heavier than expected; the prototype turboprop engine posed serious weight and placement problems, as did the drive shaft that transmitted power from the engine to the shrouded propeller. The problems were not insoluble, though, and the Aerophysics Department's gifted designer, Glen Bryant, was able to overcome them. The MARVEL flew in 1964.35

Unfortunately for the MARVEL project, its development coincided with revolutionary changes in military organization, philosophy, and technology. Between 1960 and 1963, Secretary of Defense Robert McNamara introduced new administrative techniques into Pentagon planning that had been derived from academic think tanks and schools of management. Civilian analysts trained in cost-accounting, systems analysis, and institutional management took over at the Department of Defense and in 1963 forced the armed services to describe their operations in terms of missions and the specific programs they intended to use in carrying out the missions. The services found it difficult to gain budgetary authority to undertake research projects unless they could prove that the research was directly related to a specific mission.36

Therefore, the year 1963 became a turning point in U.S. military history insofar as research was concerned. Robert McNamara's administrators used blunt instruments to define missions, and one of the casualties of their redefining was Army research on fixed-wing aircraft. Helicopters had become faster and more reliable, and the Army could more easily justify them in terms of specific missions. Helicopters quickly became the Army's main form of air transportation. Neither the Air Force nor the Navy wanted slow airplanes. Also, although over $300 million had been spent on research in vertical and short-take-off-and-landing aircraft, no V/STOL or STOL aircraft had ever become operational. The result was a winding down of research in V/STOL aircraft which meant the death of the MARVEL project. It lingered on until 1968, all the while trying to define a mission.37

The Aerophysics Department was also suffering from internal administrative stresses. Joe Cornish, a native of New Orleans, who had earned a master's degree in aeronautical engineering at Mississippi State in 1951, was named director of the Aerophysics Department the day Raspet was killed. He remained until the end of 1964, when he accepted employment in private industry. Cornish was succeeded by Sean Roberts, who had come to Mississippi State as an Irish exchange student, and who worked with Raspet as a research assistant. Roberts was an able administrator and Mel Schwartzberg, the Aerophysics Department's general manager who had come to Mississippi State with Raspet in 1948, gave Roberts most of the credit for a masterful production job and for bringing the MARVEL project to fruition. Unfortunately for Roberts, a condition of his employment was that he complete his Ph.D. in a timely fashion—something Roberts was unable to do. To make matters worse, he failed his oral examination but informed officials at Mississippi State that he had passed. When the truth finally leaked out, Dean Simrall asked Roberts to immediately turn in his keys and leave his post.

The Aerophysics Department had accomplished its goal of bringing a nationally recognized research program to Mississippi State. In 1967, it joined the Department of Aerospace Engineering to form the Department of Aerophysics and Aerospace Engineering. (Aeronautical Engineering had been renamed Aerospace Engineering in 1963.) Raspet, Cornish, and Bryant had accepted appointments in Aeronautical Engineering in 1959.[38]

Much of this improvement can be attributed to new leadership from the president's office. Ben Hilbun retired in 1960 and was succeeded by a North Carolina native, Dean Wallace Colvard, the first president without Mississippi roots. Unlike nearly all of his eleven predecessors, Colvard had followed a traditional career path for a university president, earning a Ph.D. at Purdue and serving as a department head and dean at North Carolina State University. Colvard reorganized the administration of the university, established a more formal chain of command, and brought to the university an excellent understanding of the nature of a true university, one that combined teaching and scholarship. In many ways the six years of his administration marked the end of the old university and the beginning of the new. His successor, William L. Giles, the holder of a doctorate in field crops, maintained the momentum that had been achieved toward developing a comprehensive university by establishing new graduate programs and recognizing the contribution of research to quality teaching.[39]

One of Colvard's achievements was to preside over the peaceful desegregation of the University in 1965. Governor Ross Barnett's efforts to prevent the desegregation of the University of Mississippi in 1962 had already threatened the accreditation of the College of Engineering, even though Mississippi State was not involved in the crisis. Although the Southern

Association of Schools and Colleges had accredited Mississippi State since 1926 with the exception of the Bilbo years, and had just reaccredited the university, it placed all of the public colleges and universities in the state on what it called "extra-ordinary status"—a clear warning that further political interference in the operations of Mississippi higher education would not be tolerated. Memories of the Bilbo years were quickly revived. Removal of accreditation by the Southern Association, of course, would have meant immediate withdrawal of accreditation by the ECPD and other professional associations, which required accreditation by a regional association as a prerequisite. Colvard knew that, while the threat of deaccreditation was real, it could also be used to the University's advantage as a tool to disarm the die-hard segregationists. The first black student, Richard Holmes, entered the University peacefully in the summer of 1965.[40]

Several new engineering departments and degrees emerged during the university's period of rapid expansion, even though enrollment in engineering was running counter to the general trend toward expansion. To acknowledge the complexity of the major divisions of the University the schools were renamed "colleges" in 1962. Petroleum Engineering was created in 1961, and Industrial Engineering, which had been a branch of Mechanical Engineering, became a separate department in 1962.[41] Nuclear Engineering emerged soon thereafter and G. Robert Hoke, who had worked at the Savannah River nuclear plant and the Oak Ridge Laboratories, was chosen to head the department. Nuclear Engineering immediately received a grant from the Atomic Energy Commission to begin construction of a small reactor, which the Mechanical Engineering Department agreed to build. Nuclear Engineering flourished during the boom years of the nuclear industry. In 1981 it was combined with the department of Mechanical Engineering under the leadership of C. T. Carley.[42] Chemical Engineering was moved from the Chemistry Department to Engineering in 1959. In 1960, Ceramic Engineering, later known as Ceramic and Metallurgical Engineering, began operations. Julian H. Lauchner became its head in August of that year. The department was established to take advantage of funding opportunities provided by the armed services and NASA. Both the military and the space agency were interested in the sponsoring research on the behavior of polycrystalline materials under extremes of temperature and stress. Although Ceramic and Metallurgical Engineering obtained several research grants from federal agencies, the department attracted few students and underwent restructuring in 1969 to form a new department of Materials Engineering.[43] Biological Engineering came into existence in 1967, under the administrative umbrella of the Agricultural Engineering Department.[44]

We have seen that engineering employment in the United States since World War II has been both highly cyclical and dramatically conditioned by national technological priorities, which, in turn have been driven by politics. Traditionally, engineering students have been especially sensitive to their prospects for immediate employment upon graduation, with enrollment in engineering education generally reflecting the demand for engineers generated by national programs.

Thus, the expansion of the Cold War in the 1950s, the race to land on the moon in the 1960s, and the emergence of the computer as a major factor in military and civilian technological change greatly affected schools of engineering. Enrollment at Mississippi State followed these national trends—reaching a high point of 1,705 students in 1958, before falling to 1,238 in 1962. The space race caused more students to be attracted to the College of Engineering, which reached an enrollment of 1,698 in 1967, only to crash the next year due to a drastic reduction in government spending and a "chain reaction throughout industry." Enrollment fell until it reached a level of 1070 in 1973, when enrollment began another gradual increase until 1958 levels were passed in the late 1970s. Enrollment reached 1936 in 1979.[45]

In a way, the decreases in enrollment during the 1960s and 70s were beneficial because they gave the College a welcome respite from constantly trying to cope with understaffing and overcrowding. The respite also provided an opportunity to catch up with the rest of the nation in terms of salaries, equipment, and teaching conditions. Expenditures for faculty salaries rose from $365,245 in 1959-60, to $555,710 in 1962-63, even though enrollment fell by more than 25 percent. During the same period the number of budgeted faculty members rose by over 60 percent to forty-four. The rise in enrollment during the 1960s was accompanied by an increase in salary budgets, to $998,564, and an increase in budgeted positions to sixty-two. During the crash of the next five years, the salary budget rose to $1,494,786, while the number of faculty members increased to eighty-four. By 1979, the budget had increased to $2,583,874 for ninety-six faculty members.[46]

The increased state support of higher education that began with the arrival of the baby-boom generation on campus allowed the College of Engineering to improve the professional qualifications of the faculty, expand research programs, and improve facilities. These improvements meant that problems in retaining accreditation gradually disappeared. The accreditation visit in 1964 resulted in a much-improved report. Aerospace and Chemical Engineering received four-year accreditation, while Civil and Electrical Engineering received the coveted full six-year accreditation. In 1968, the ECPD commended the College for the progress it had made since the last accreditation visit, praising it for the efforts it had made in upgrading the curriculum, adding quality faculty, and increasing research and scholarship. The ECPD also applauded the University for its improved support services, library funding, and computer facilities. As usual, the ECPD criticized the College of Engineering for its inability to attract senior faculty with broad teaching, research, and industrial experience, a failing which the ECPD attributed to uncompetitive faculty salaries. By 1972, the ECPD again commended the college for its progress in improving salaries, decreasing teaching loads, and improving research programs. Four years later the ECPD approved full six-year accreditation for nine of the ten engineering departments, criticizing the College only for insufficient research. In general, the accreditation inspections made since 1976 have been positive and supportive, and the sense of near-desperation that marked many earlier accreditation visits has disappeared.[47]

When Harry Simrall retired in 1978 and turned the leadership of the College over to Willie L. McDaniel he left a college that was vastly different from the unit he had begun to lead in 1957. From Walker to Flinsch, deans of the college had led a unit almost entirely devoted to undergraduate teaching. Few faculty members possessed advanced degrees, teaching loads were enormous, and salaries were abysmal. Most faculty members knew little of current advances in their professions because they were professionally isolated and research was almost nonexistent. Retaining ECPD accreditation was always a worry; most ECPD visits resulted in accreditation for the minimum periods. Although student enrollment grew constantly, there were never enough classrooms or laboratories to house them adequately.

By 1978, the situation had improved dramatically. Whereas Dean McDaniel knew that the College of Engineering still faced some "perilous times," the general situation was better than it had ever been before. For the first time, the maximum level of accreditation had nearly been achieved. Funding obtained in the 1960s provided for such buildings as the Patterson engineering laboratories, the Ethridge Chemical Engineering building, and the

Walker engineering laboratories. The Simrall electrical engineering building, authorized in 1975, further eased overcrowding. The number of faculty positions had tripled and, although inflation had decreased the value of the dollar, the amounts budgeted for faculty salaries had increased sixfold. Although enrollments had gyrated dramatically in line with national technology programs, student enrollment had returned nearly to the 2,000-student level where it stabilized and then began to grow.

Outside support in the form of gifts and grants was increasing which indicated to Harry Simrall that the college's reputation in engineering circles throughout the United States was improving. Most important, while quality undergraduate teaching remained a top priority, research had become a vital part of academic life for Mississippi State engineers. The College had passed its nearby competitors in terms of research expenditures per faculty member. By 1980, Mississippi State led Vanderbilt, and the Universities of Mississippi, South Carolina, and Alabama in its research expenditures per faculty member and was only a small amount behind Tennessee, Auburn, and LSU. "It appears," wrote Simrall in his last annual report, "that the engineering research program is well on its way to becoming a major activity in the College of Engineering."[48]

The main events in the history of the College of Engineering during the past two decades have been the establishment of internationally recognized research programs. During the 1974-75 academic year, the Department of Aerophysics and Aerospace Engineering took stock of its strengths and decided to concentrate its research in three major areas. (1) technology related to general aviation aircraft, to be led by E. J. Cross, who was succeeded by George Bennett in 1979; (2) computational fluid dynamics (CFD) to be led by Joe F. Thompson; (3) magnetohydrodynamics (MHD), with special emphasis on energy production from coal, led by David L. Murphree. This concentration of energy was astonishingly prescient and these three research areas have been major contributors in Mississippi State's effort to gain an international reputation for engineering research.[49]

The MHD program began in the late 1960s with a series of small grants from the National Science Foundation to conduct basic research in magnetohydrodynamics. Murphree had worked with the Raspet group as an undergraduate research assistant for four years, conducting award-winning research in fluid dynamics, and had graduated in 1960. Later, he received a Ph.D. degree from the University of Wisconsin, and returned to Mississippi

State as a faculty member.⁵⁰ Basically, magnetohydrodynamics involves generating electricity from burning fuel without using a generator. In basic form, MHD electricity generation takes place by burning pulverized coal in a special chamber. The superheated gases produced pass at high speed through a channel containing a magnetic field where they are "seeded" with potassium salt which makes the plasma conductive. The magnetic field traps free electrons which are removed by electrodes, thus producing electricity. The remaining gasses then can be used to produce steam, which generates electricity in the conventional manner. By combining these two methods the efficiency of electrical generation can be dramatically increased.⁵¹

Murphree's choice of a research area was fortunate. When the energy crisis began with the Arab oil embargo in 1972 Murphree was in an excellent position to take advantage of national initiatives to find alternative forms of energy. In 1976, the Energy Research and Development Administration (ERDA) selected Mississippi State—along with MIT, Stanford, and the University of Tennessee Space Institute—as a research center for MHD technology. ERDA began providing the newly established MHD Energy Center with some $300,000 per year. Mississippi State assumed responsibility for developing diagnostic instruments that could measure and evaluate the internal functions of a MHD combuster in operation, as well as developing computer control systems for MHD facilities. The university also undertook studies in theoretical modelling. By 1980, the Department of Energy had provided Mississippi State with over $4 million dollars in funding—by far the largest amount ever received for a research project. Eight years later the MHD Energy Center, which had become a research unit separate from the College of Engineering, changed its name to the Diagnostic Instrumentation and Analysis Laboratory (DIAL) and continued to receive large amounts of federal support for its research. Under the direction of Steve Shepard, the center had received over $30 million by 1990 and was utilizing the talent of some sixty faculty members from the colleges of Engineering and Arts and Sciences to complete research in a variety of areas.⁵²

The research program in CFD also began with the pioneering efforts of a Mississippi State graduate who had worked with the Aerophysics group. Joe Thompson had earned a master's degree under Joe Cornish in 1963, and, after working on the Apollo project at the Marshall Space Flight Center, he returned to Mississippi State with a Ph.D. degree from the Georgia Institute of Technology where he had written a dissertation on CFD. Essentially, CFD involves mathematically simulating the flow of fluids around moving bodies. To understand CFD one can imagine a room filled with an extremely large number of points which are all linked mathematically by partial differential equations. When a body passes through the room the physical forces imposed on the points by changes in velocity, pressure, and temperature cause their values to change which, in turn, alters their relationship to the other points in the room. Thus, to model the changes imposed on the space, billions of equations must be solved simultaneously. This can be done only with the most powerful of computers. A key to this modeling is "numerical grid generation," which involves distributing these points in such a way as to allow efficient solutions of real-world problems such as modeling the surfaces of aircraft.

Like Murphree, Thompson had begun basic research in an area with enormous potential long before it became fashionable. Together with two colleagues, Z. U. A. Warsi and Wayne Mastin, he wrote the only textbook in the field, and with the aid of David Whitfield obtained grant support from the Defense Advanced Research Projects Administration (DARPA). Mississippi State's research program achieved a major boost in 1978 when Donald Trotter, a Mississippi State graduate and a very successful Silicon Valley electrical engineer and executive, returned to the University. The University had decided to embark on a new engineering research program that revolved around designing custom electronic circuits required mainly for military and aerospace applications. An enhancement to the program came in 1988 when the departments of aerospace and electrical engineering received $300,000 worth of circuit boards from Sun Microsystems to assist in the development of a special purpose computer dedicated to solving CFD problems. The donation, together with DARPA funding, led to the construction of the Mapped Array Differential Equations Machine (MADEM) which could solve CFD problems faster than the best supercomputers. MADEM brought the microelectronics group and the CFD group together and helped gain Mississippi State national and international recognition for research in electrical and aerospace engineering.[53]

In the spring of 1987, the work of the two groups was recognized by an invitation to write a proposal for funding to establish an independent research center in the area. With the help of Senator John Stennis, the U.S. Air Force Office of Scientific Research supplied $5 million to create the new Research Center for Advanced Scientific Computing in Mississippi State's new research park, with an additional $500,000 to equip it. By this time David Murphree had left DIAL to become director of a new Institute for Technological Development (ITD), established by Congress to help Mississippi become competitive in high-technology areas.54

The third research area involved more traditional kinds of aeronautical engineering at the Raspet research laboratories, where work on improving the efficiency of aircraft continued. In 1981 George Bennett, director of the Raspet laboratory, received funding from Lockheed Corporation to conduct advanced flight tests using a modified sailplane. In order to achieve prolonged flight times a sophisticated sailplane was modified by adding a small jet engine to it. Once airborne the craft could remain in flight for extended periods of time. One of the main purposes of the project was to study the effect of "spanwise blowing" on aircraft. In a series of experiments August Raspet would have been proud of, a blower forced air across the wings which greatly increased lift at high angles of attack. The sailplane was also used to study the effects of deformations in the wings and to determine methods of noise reduction. The Raspet group was able to revive interest in the MARVEL (which had been put in storage after its funding ran out.) The energy crisis revived interest in aircraft efficiency which manufacturers had largely ignored during the years of cheap fuel, and it flew once more. "This is the shape airplanes of the future will have to have, thanks to the cost of the fuel," said George Bennett in 1981, citing the many design innovations incorporated in MARVEL. "We're going to lose out on aviation's future if we don't move on this front," he continued, "just the way Detroit is losing out to Japan now [in automobile manufacturing.]"55

It was ironic that Bennett should have said what he did about Japan because the development of a close cooperative relationship with the Honda Corporation, one of Japan's leading manufacturers, proved to be the Aerophysics group's most fruitful research initiative. In 1986, the Raspet Labs entered into an agreement with the Honda Research and Development Company to undertake research focused on developing fuel-efficient, aerodynamically sound aircraft built with composite materials. When the initial grant was announced, Nobuhiko Kawamoto, President of Honda Research and Development, said: "Honda is beginning what is hoped to be a long relationship with Mississippi State University." The cooperative relationship between Honda engineers and Mississippi State University faculty members was a productive one, and in 1989 the president of Honda Motor Company brought a $1 million gift to the College of Engineering to be used for engineering scholarships. Later that year, Honda announced that it wished to erect a $4 million research building near the Raspet Flight Research Laboratory. The building was to be used for composite materials research and would revert to Mississippi State when Honda's research was completed in the late 1990s.[56]

Willie McDaniel resigned as dean of the College of Engineering in 1988, to become associate vice president for academic affairs at Mississippi State. He was succeeded by Robert Altenkirch who had previously been chairman of the Department of Mechanical Engineering at the University of Kentucky. Altenkirch soon found that he would be involved in helping the College of Engineering reach a milestone in its history through designation as a National Science Foundation Engineering Research Center. In 1988, Joe Thompson, David Whitfield, and Donald Trotter submitted a proposal to the NSF to establish the center, and the proposal received favorable reviews. The NSF scheduled a site visit in June 1989 which was successful, and after several months of anxious waiting to see whether Congress would provide NSF with adequate funds, Thompson received notice, in January 1990, that Mississippi State had been made an Engineering Research Center for Computational Field Simulation. Mississippi State's proposal was one of three funded in 1990, allowing it to join a select group that included only eighteen other centers around the United States.[57]

The Engineering Research Center was dedicated on May 10, 1991 by the new director of the National Science Foundation, Walter E. Massey, a native of Mississippi. Massey spoke of the experience of viewing Mississippi from the outside and how pleased he had been to see the emergence of a new culture in the state that recognized that research "is vital to education and to economic progress." The ERC, he concluded, "exemplifies the benefits of this new culture and the potential that exists in the state." With these comments he was indirectly recognizing the contributions of generations of Mississippi State faculty members whose calls for investment in higher education and research so often seemed to be lost in the wind.[58]

Notes

CHAPTER ONE: *Establishing the Mechanical Feature*

1. David Madsen, "The Land-Grant University: Myth and Reality," in G. Lester Anderson, ed., *Land-Grant Universities and Their Continuing Challenge* (East Lansing, Michigan: Michigan State University Press, 1976) pp. 23-30.

2. Edward D. Eddy, Jr., *The Land-Grant Movement: A Capsule History of the Educational Revolution Which Established Colleges for All the People* (Washington, D.C.: American Association of Land-Grant Universities, 1962), p. 19.

3. George P. Sanger, *Statutes at Large, Treaties, and Proclamations of the United States of America from December 5, 1859 to March 3, 1863*, 12 (Boston: Little, Brown, 1863) 503; David G. Sansing, *Making Haste Slowly: The Troubled History of Higher Education in Mississippi* (Jackson: University Press of Mississippi, 1990), p. 63.

4. Allen Cabaniss, *The University of Mississippi: Its First Hundred Years*, 2d ed. (Hattiesburg: University and College Press of Mississippi, 1971), p. 29; Sansing, *Making Haste Slowly*. pp. 41, 60-61.

5. Sansing, *Making Haste Slowly*, p. 41.

6. Sansing, *Making Haste Slowly*, pp. 60-61; John K. Bettersworth, *People's University: The Centennial History of Mississippi State* (Jackson: University Press of Mississippi, 1980), p. 4.

7. Stephen D. Lee, *The Agricultural and Mechanical College of Mississippi* (Jackson, Miss.: Clarion-Ledger Publishing House, 1889), pp. 7-8; John C. Hardy to G.B.R. Henderson, July 3, 1909, Hardy Papers, Correspondence, Agronomy-Alford, Mississippi State University Archives; hereafter abbreviated MSUA.

8. *The Comet* (Jackson, Miss.), August 2, 1879.

9. Many people are under the impression that the funds provided by the Morrill land-grant legislation were massive in scope. In truth, the land-grant program was quite small when compared to other land-giveaway programs

the federal government engaged in during the nineteenth century, or to the costs involved in operating a college or university. The Morrill Act provided seventeen million acres of land for the purpose of higher education, a figure almost insignificant when compared with the 234 million acres given away as a result of the Homestead Act and the 181 million acres given to the transcontinental railroads. Mississippi sold its lands for ninety cents an acre, which, with interest, had risen to a total of $227,150 by 1878. Mississippi Agricultural and Mechanical College's share of these funds was $113,575, which, invested at 5 percent interest, yielded $5,678.75 per year, hardly a princely sum even in 1878. Alcorn University was established in 1871 and had originally been allotted three-fifths of the land-grant funds. Under the 1878 reorganization plan, however, its share of the funds was reduced to one-half, even though the black population of Mississippi was considerably greater than the white population. Madsen, "Land-Grant University," p. 32; Sansing, *Making Haste Slowly*, pp. 63-64.

10. "An Act to establish and organize Agricultural and Mechanical Colleges, and to regulate the government of same," *General Laws of Mississippi, 1878*, chap. 19, pp. 118-23; *Second Annual Catalog of the Officers and Students of the Agricultural and Mechanical College of Mississippi, 1881-82* (Jackson, Miss.: the Clarion Steam Publishing House, 1881), p. 15. Throughout the history of Mississippi State University, catalogs have been given titles with slightly different wordings and have been produced by printers in different locations. Hereafter, all are referred to as *Catalog*. All are available in the Mississippi State University Archives.

11. Bettersworth, *People's University*, pp. 8-10.

12. Herman Hattaway, *General Stephen D. Lee* (Jackson: University Press of Mississippi, 1976), p. 3; Bettersworth, *People's University*, p. 22.

13. Bettersworth, *People's University*, p. 23, quoting an unidentified newspaper clipping in a scrapbook assembled by Blewitt Lee, S. D. Lee's son.

14. Madsen, "Land-Grant University," p. 35; Sansing, *Making Haste Slowly*, p. 65.

15. Bettersworth, *People's University*, pp. 22-25.

16. *The Comet*, October 16, 1880.

17. S. D. Lee to Put Darden, master of the State Grange, December 4, 1884, S. D. Lee Correspondence, MSUA.

18. Sansing, *Making Haste Slowly*, p. 66; Bettersworth, *People's University*, p. 28; *Catalog*, 1889-90, p. 12.

19. *Catalog*, 1881-82, frontispiece.

20. Ibid., p. 17.

21. Ibid., p. 27.
22. *Catalog,* 1882-83, p. 31.
23. *Catalog,* 1884-85, p. 41.
24. *Biennial Report of the Trustees, President and Other Officers of the Agricultural and Mechanical College of Mississippi for the Years 1884-85* (Jackson, Miss.: Clarion Steam Publishing House, 1885), p. 72. These reports were published with slightly different titles and by a variety of publishers between 1883 and 1941, when they first appeared on an annual basis. Hereafter, they have been shortened to *Biennial Report* or *Annual Report.* All are available in the Mississippi State University Archives; Bettersworth, *People's University,* pp. 92-93; Lee responded to his critics with a spirited defense of Mississippi A & M, pointing out that the institution had clearly served the needs of the agricultural and industrial classes and had in no way "interfered with the attendance of students at Oxford." Lee, *Agricultural and Mechanical College,* pp. 10, 16-17.
25. Madsen, "Land-Grant University," p. 35.
26. *Catalog,* 1889-90, p. 13; Bettersworth, *People's University,* pp. 92-98.
27. *Biennial Report,* 1888-89, pp. 3-8.
28. Ibid., pp. 8-13.
29 *Catalog,* 1890-91, p. 35.
30. *The Statutes at Large of the United States of America from December, 1889, to March, 1891,* 26 (Washington, D.C.: Government Printing Office, 1891). 418.
31. *Biennial Report,* 1890-91, pp. 3-20.
32. Lee, *Agricultural and Mechanical College,* p. 7.
33. *Catalog,* 1890-91, p. 30; *Biennial Report,* 1890-91, pp. 6-7.
34. Harry Gwinner to S. D. Lee, April 19, 1892, annual report of the Department of Mechanic Arts, MSUA; *Catalog,* 1892-93, p. 36.
35. *Catalog,* 1891-92, pp. 30-31; *Catalog,* 1892-93, p. 31. Most likely, this graduate program existed primarily as a device that allowed the college to keep recent graduates on campus who could serve as teaching assistants.
36. *Catalog,* 1891-92, pp. 35-36.
37. *Biennial Report,* 1890-91, p. 31.
38. *Catalog,* 1892-93, p. 36.
39. *Catalog,* 1891-92, pp. 29-30.
40. Harry Gwinner to S. D. Lee, June 7, 1893, annual report of the Department of Mechanic Arts, MSUA; *Catalog,* 1890-91, p. 23.
41. Harry Gwinner to S. D. Lee, June 6, 1892; and Gwinner to S. D. Lee, May 21, 1894, annual reports of the Department of Mechanic Arts, MSUA.

42. Harry Gwinner to S. D. Lee, June 7, 1893, annual report of the Department of Mechanic Arts, MSUA.

43. Ibid.

44. *The Engineer: His Preparation and Work, Special Bulletin of the School of Engineering, 1929* (State College: Mississippi A & M, 1929), pp. 11-12.

45. Harry Gwinner to S. D. Lee, June 7, 1893, annual report of the Department of Mechanic Arts, MSUA.

46. A. J. Weichardt to S. D. Lee, June 5, 1895, annual report of the Department of Mechanic Arts, MSUA.

47. *Biennial Report*, 1894-96, p. 8.

48. *Catalog*, 1899-1900, pp. 65-67; *Biennial Report*, 1898-99, p. 29.

49. *Catalog*, 1898-99, pp. 36-37.

50. *Biennial Report*, 1898-99, p. 10.

51. *Catalog*, 1900-1901, pp. 38-39; *Biennial Report*, 1900-1901, p. 50.

52. *Biennial Report*, 1896-98, p. 8.

53. *Catalog*, 1895-96 pp. 44-45; *Biennial Report*, 1894-96, p. 7; *Biennial Report*, 1897-99, p. 30.

CHAPTER TWO: *The Challenges of Growth*

1. John K. Bettersworth, *People's University: The Centennial History of Mississippi State* (Jackson: University Press of Mississippi, 1980), p. 112.

2. Bettersworth, *People's University*, p. 115.

3. C. E. Ard to J. C. Hardy [1902], J. C. Hardy Correspondence, Ames-Ard, 1904, MSUA.

4. *Catalog*, 1899-1900, p. 75; B. M. Walker, Special Report Concerning School of Engineering, n.d. [1902], filed with annual and Biennial reports, MSUA.

5. Bettersworth, *People's University*, p. 125; Walker, Special Report.

6. *Inaugural Addresses of the Governors of Mississippi, 1890-1980* (Oxford: Bureau of Governmental Research, 1980), pp. 13-14, 16.

7. A. J. Weichardt to J. C. Hardy, May 1, 1902, annual report of the Department of Mechanical Arts and Electricity; Albert Barnes to J. C. Hardy, May 6, 1903, report of the Mechanical Engineering Department; and C. E. Ard to J. C. Hardy, November 1, 1903, annual report of the Department of Physics and Electrical Engineering; C. E. Ard to J. C. Hardy, May 9, 1904, annual report of the Department of Physics and Electrical Engineering, MSUA.

8. *Biennial Report*, 1904-1905, p. 42; *Catalog, 1905-1906*, pp. 219-

30; C. E. Ard to J. C. Hardy, May 1, 1905, annual report of the Department of Physics and Electrical Engineering, MSUA.

9. C. E. Ard to J. C. Hardy, November 1, 1907, biennial report of the Department of Physics and Electrical Engineering; C. E. Ard to J. C. Hardy, May 1, 1908, annual report of the Department of Physics and Electrical Engineering, MSUA.

10. Albert Barnes to J. C. Hardy, May 14, 1907, Hardy Correspondence, Bradford-Breach, 1907, MSUA.

11. Albert Barnes to J. C. Hardy, May 6, 1903, annual report of the Mechanical Engineering Department; C. E. Ard to J. C. Hardy, November 1, 1903, May 9, 1904, annual reports of the Department of Physics and Electrical Engineering; Albert Barnes to J. C. Hardy, October 4, 1903, biennial report of the Department of Mechanical Engineering, MSUA.

12. C. E. Ard to J. C. Hardy, November 1, 1903, biennial report of the Department of Physics and Electrical Engineering; B. M. Walker to J. C. Hardy, March 10, 1903, Hardy Papers, Walcutt-Westall, MSUA.

13. *Biennial Report*, 1905, p. 46; *Bulletin of the Mississippi Agricultural and Mechanical College: School of Engineering* (Agricultural College, Miss.: Mississippi Agricultural and Mechanical College, 1904), p. 14.

14. *Biennial Report*, 1904-1905, p. 44.

15. *Bulletin of the School of Engineering*, pp. 4-7; *Biennial Report*, 1905, p. 49.

16. *Bulletin of the School of Engineering*, pp. 8-9.

17. J. W. Fox to J. C. Hardy, October 27, 1903, annual report of the Department of Civil and Rural Engineering, MSUA; *Biennial Report*, 1904-1905, pp. 27, 29; *Bulletin of the School of Engineering*, pp. 11-13; *Biennial Report*, 1901, p. 30.

18. *Starkville News*, March 13, 1908.

19. William F. Holmes, *The White Chief: James Kimble Vardaman* (Baton Rouge: Louisiana State University Press, 1970), pp. 91, 117.

20. C. E. Ard to J. C. Hardy, May 1, 1907, annual report of the Department of Physics and Electrical Engineering; C. E. Ard to J. C. Hardy, n.d., annual report of the Department of Physics and Electrical Engineering, MSUA.

21. C. E. Ard to J. C. Hardy, May 1, 1907, Annual Report of the Department of Physics and Electrical Engineering, MSUA.

22. C. E. Ard to J. C. Hardy, May 1, 1906, annual report of the Department of Physics and Electrical Engineering; C. E. Ard to J. C. Hardy, November 1, 1907, biennial report of the Department of Physics and Electrical Engineering, MSUA.

23. J. C. Hardy press release, January 16, 1908, Vertical File, MSU History, MSUA.

24. Charles Hancock to J. C. Hardy, May 6, 1908, annual report of the Department of Civil Engineering and Drawing; B. M. Walker to J. C. Hardy, May 6, 1909, annual report of the School of Engineering, MSUA; *Starkville News*, July 24, 1908.

25. Bettersworth, *People's University*, p. 158, *Starkville News*, February 2, 1912.

26. *Starkville News*, February 2, 1912.

27. B. M. Walker to J. C. Hardy, May 23, 1912, annual report of the School of Engineering, MSUA.

28. C. E. Ard to J. C. Hardy, December 14, 1911, filed with annual and biennial reports; R. C. Carpenter to George R. Hightower, June 10, 1913, annual report of the Department of Mechanical Engineering; Clarence E. Reid to G. R. Hightower, June 18, 1913, biennial report of the Department of Electrical Engineering, MSUA; *Biennial Report*, 1912-13, p. 161.

29. *Biennial Report*, 1910-11, pp. 211-13; *Biennial Report*, 1912-13, pp. 160-61; R. C. Carpenter to George Hightower, June 10, 1913, MSUA.

30. *Biennial Report*, 1910-11, p. 212; Clarence E. Reid to G. R. Hightower, June 16, 1913, biennial report of the Department of Electrical Engineering, MSUA.

31. D. W. Brown to J. C. Hardy, April 30, 1910, annual report of the Department of Civil Engineering and Drawing, MSUA.

32. *Biennial Report*, 1912-13, p. 164.

33. *Biennial Report*, 1912-13, pp. 153-54; Clarence Reid to J. C. Hardy, May 20, 1911, annual report of the Department of Physics and Electrical Engineering, MSUA.

34. Clarence Reid to G. R. Hightower, May 1, 1914, annual report of the Department of Electrical Engineering, MSUA.

35. Clarence Reid to G. R. Hightower, May 3, 1913, annual report of the Department of Electrical Engineering, MSUA.

36. C. E. Ard to J. C. Hardy, December 14, 1911, filed with annual and biennial reports, MSUA.

37. Clarence Reid to J. C. Hardy, n.d. [December 1911], filed with annual and biennial reports, MSUA.

38. Clarence Reid to G. R. Hightower, May 1, 1914, annual report of the Department of Electrical Engineering, MSUA.

39. Lucius L. Patterson to W. H. Smith, May 15, 1920, annual report of the Department of Electrical Engineering, MSUA.

40. *Biennial Report*, 1910-11, p. 217; *Biennial Report*, 1912-13, pp.

163-64; C. E. Ard to J. C. Hardy, n.d. [1909], annual report of the Department of Physics and Electrical Engineering, MSUA.

41. Clarence Reid to J. C. Hardy, n.d. [December 1911], filed with annual and biennial reports, MSUA.

42. *Biennial Report,* 1912-13, pp. 153-60.

43. *Biennial Report,* 1912-13, pp. 149-50; Clarence Reid to G. R. Hightower, May 1, 1914, annual report of the Department of Electrical Engineering; Robert Gay to G. R. Hightower, June 14, 1913, biennial report of the Department of Civil Engineering and Drawing, MSUA.

44. *Biennial Report,* 1912-13, p. 150; L. L. Patterson to W. H. Smith, May 15, 1918, annual report of the Department of Electrical Engineering, MSUA.

45. C. E. Ard to J. C. Hardy, May 2, 1910, annual report of the Department of Physics and Electrical Engineering; Clarence Reid to J. C. Hardy, May 20, 1911, annual report of the Department of Physics and Electrical Engineering, MSUA.

46. Clarence Reid to G. R. Hightower, May 1, 1914, annual report of the Department of Electrical Engineering, MSUA.

47. Robert Gay to G. R. Hightower, April 15, 1915, annual report of the Department of Civil Engineering and Drawing, MSUA.

48. *Biennial Report,* 1912-13, pp. 28-29.

49. Robert Gay to G. R. Hightower, May 10, 1916, annual report of the Department of Civil Engineering and Drawing, MSUA.

50. Robert Gay to G. R. Hightower, April 30, 1914, annual report of the Department of Civil Engineering and Drawing, MSUA; the Carnegie Foundation's influential report on the state of American medical education was Abraham Flexner, *Medical Education in the United States and Canada,* bulletin no. 4 (New York: Carnegie Foundation for the Advancement of Teaching, 1910). The impact of the report was devastating—by 1915, 92 of 155 medical schools had closed their doors. Brown, *Rockefeller Medicine Men* (Berkeley: University of California Press, 1979), p. 147.

51. *Starkville News,* August 18, 1916.

CHAPTER THREE: *The Struggle for Survival*

1. *Biennial Report,* 1918-19, pp. 63, 119; *Starkville News,* May 11, 1917.

2. T. G. Gladney to W. H. Smith, June 26, 1917, biennial report of the Department of Civil Engineering and Drawing, MSUA.

3. John K. Bettersworth, *People's University: The Centennial History*

of Mississippi State (Jackson: University Press of Mississippi, 1980), p. 190; J. Wendell Bailey, *The Mississippi A & M College and the War* (Brandon, Miss.: Mississippi A & M Bureau of War Records, n.d. [1921]), pp. 142-43; "Shop talk: Official Organization Bulletin of the Mississippi A & M College," December 22-January 10, 1917; *Biennial Report*, 1918-19, pp. 14, 76.

4. *Biennial Report*, 1918-19, p. 66.

5. *Biennial Report*, 1918-19, p. 63; E. R. Gross to B. M. Walker, July 1, 1921, biennial report of the Division of Agricultural Engineering, MSUA.

6. Bettersworth, *People's University*, pp. 125, 139-40.

7. *Biennial Report*, 1920-21, pp. 26, 36; E. R. Gross to B. M. Walker, July 1, 1921, biennial report of the Division of Agricultural Engineering, MSUA; *Catalog*, 1920-21, p. 61.

8. *Catalog*, 1914-15, pp. 92-95.

9. E. R. Gross to B. M. Walker, July 1, 1921, biennial report of the Division of Agricultural Engineering, MSUA.

10. *Biennial Report*, 1920-21, pp. 1-8.

11. *Biennial Report*, 1918-19, p. 68; Bettersworth, *People's University*, pp. 191-92.

12. *Biennial Report*, 1918-19, pp. 67-74.

13. *Biennial Report*, 1920-21, pp. 3-6; *Biennial Report*, 1924-25, p. 10.

14. *Biennial Report*, 1922-23, pp. 5-6; "A & M Starkville: Academic and Library Building," n.d., records of the State Bond Improvement Commission, Record Group 20, August 16, 1922–November 3, 1922, Archives of the State of Mississippi, Jackson, Miss.

15. Mildred Barr, "History of the Engineering School at Mississippi State College," typescript, n.d. [1957], MSUA.

16. Barr, "History of Engineering School."

17. L. L. Patterson to B. M. Walker, June 30, 1923, biennial report of the Department of Electrical Engineering, MSUA. The renovated building is now McCain Hall.

18. B. M. Walker to D. C. Hull, July 8, 1921, biennial report of the School of Engineering, MSUA.

19. *Catalog*, 1919-20, pp. 68-69.

20. Matthew L. Freeman to D. C. Hull, June 15, 1921, annual report of the Department of Architectural Engineering and Drawing; Matthew L. Freeman to B. M. Walker, June 19, 1923, biennial report of the Department of Architectural Engineering and Drawing; B. M. Walker to D. C. Hull, May 15, 1923, annual report of the School of Engineering, MSUA.

21. *Starkville News*, July 7, 1922.

22. T. G. Gladney to B. M. Walker, June 30, 1923, annual report of the Department of Civil Engineering; Matthew Freeman to B. M. Walker, June 19, 1923, biennial report of the Department of Architectural Engineering and Drawing; H. W. Moody to B. M. Walker, June 15, 1927, biennial report of the School of Engineering, MSUA.

23. *The Mississippi A & M Alumnus: A Biographical Directory of the Faculty*, 4:2-3 (January-April 1924).

24. B. M. Walker to Roy Barnhill, June 22, 1925, Walker Correspondence; H. W. Moody to B. M. Walker, June 15, 1927, biennial report of the School of Engineering, MSUA.

25. T. G. Gladney to B. M. Walker, June 21, 1927, filed with annual and biennial reports; L. L. Patterson to B. M. Walker, August 10, 1925, biennial report of the Department of Electrical Engineering; L. L. Patterson to B. M. Walker, July 15, 1929, biennial report of the Department of Electrical Engineering, MSUA; *Starkville News*, December 24, 1925.

26. Walker's fame rested on his dissertation, "The Resolution of Higher Singularities of Algebraic Curves into Ordinary Nodes." Buz Walker, Vertical File, MSUA; 1939 typescript biography of Walker in the possession of Mrs. Nancy Walker.

27. *Biennial Report*, 1912-13, p. 144; B. M. Walker to C. C. Sandez, March 10, 1926, Walker Correspondence, MSUA.

28. Bettersworth, *People's University*, pp. 196-98; Biennial Report, 1926-27, pp. 7-8; *Catalog*, 1928-29, p. 61; B. M. Walker to H. B. Campbell, August 16, 1926; D. M. Key, president, Association of College and Secondary Schools of the Southern States, to B. M. Walker, July 23, 1926. C. R. Mann, director, American Council on Education, to B. M. Walker, August 26, 1926, Walker Correspondence, MSUA.

29. B. M. Walker to _____ Slaughter, August 9, 1926; B. M. Walker to the Executive Council of Tau Beta Pi, November 12, 1927, Walker Correspondence, MSUA; A. G. Holmes, *A Short History of the Mechanical Engineering Department of Mississippi State University of Agriculture and Applied Sciences, 1892-1976* (Mississippi State: Department of Mechanical Engineering, 1976), pp. 39-43; Buz Walker, "Fifty Years," p. 8, manuscript in Walker Vertical File, MSUA.

30. David G. Sansing, *Making Haste Slowly: The Troubled History of Higher Education in Mississippi* (Jackson: University Press of Mississippi, 1990), pp. 81, 84; Bettersworth, *People's University*, pp. 159, 178, 192; William F. Holmes, *The White Chief: James Kimble Vardaman* (Baton Rouge: Louisiana State University Press, 1970), pp. 167-75.

31. Michael V. O'Shea, *A State Educational System at Work* (n.p.: The

Bernard B. Jones Fund, 1927); *Inaugural Addressess of the Governors of Mississippi: 1890-1980* (Oxford, Miss.: Bureau of Governmental Research, 1980), pp. 146-47.

32. Sansing, *Making Haste Slowly,* pp. 91-102, 104-105.

33. Bettersworth, *People's University,* p. 208; Walker, "Fifty Years," p. 7.

34. *Biennial Report,* 1930-31, p. 11; Bettersworth, *People's University,* p. 210; Walker, "Fifty Years," p. 8.

35. *Jackson (Miss.) Daily News,* October 4, 1930.

36. L. L. Patterson to Hugh Critz, June 1, 1932, annual report of the School of Engineering, MSUA; *Biennial Report,* 1932-33, p. 12; L. L. Patterson to A. B. Butts, May 15, 1934, annual report of the School of Engineering, MSUA; A. G. Holmes, *Short History,* p. 29; *Starkville News,* March 20, 1931.

37. *Biennial Report,* 1932-33, p. 5.

38. Bettersworth, *People's University,* pp. 213-14; L. L. Patterson, "Survey of Departmental Needs," May 1932, file 13, Budget Commission, Office of the Dean of Engineering; L. L. Patterson to Hugh Critz, July 1, 1931, biennial report of the Department of Mechanical Engineering; R. C. Carpenter to L. L. Patterson, May 13, 1933, recommendations for Department of Mathematics; Dewey McCain to Hugh Critz and L. L. Patterson, May 15, 1933, biennial report of the Department of Civil Engineering; L. L. Patterson to Hugh Critz, May 19, 1933, annual report of the School of Engineering, MSUA.

39. *Biennial Report,* 1932-33, pp. 6-7; M. L. Freeman to Hugh Critz, May 31, 1932, biennial report of the Department of Drawing; Dewey McCain to L. L. Patterson, June 26, 1933, letter filed with annual and biennial reports, MSUA. The board of trustees later made up the unpaid salaries at a rate of seventy-five cents to the dollar. Bettersworth, *People's University,* p. 215.

40. *Biennial Report,* 1932-33, pp. 49-51.

41. Sansing, *Making Haste Slowly,* p. 114; Frank P. Bachman, *Report of Functions of State Institutions of Higher Learning Mississippi: A Basis for the Allocation of Funds* (Nashville, Tenn.: George Peabody College for Teachers, 1933).

42. Bettersworth, *People's University,* pp. 222-24.

43. Bettersworth, *People's University,* p. 223.

44. Minutes of the Board of Trustees of the Institutions of Higher Learning, January 23, 1933. Hereafter abbreviated IHL.

CHAPTER FOUR: *Toward National Recognition*

1. L. L. Patterson to A. B. Butts, May 15, 1934, annual report of the School of Engineering; R. C. Carpenter to Hugh Critz, May 12, 1934, annual report of the Department of Mechanical Engineering, MSUA.

2. R. C. Carpenter to Hugh Critz, May 12, 1934, annual report of the Department of Mechanical Engineering, MSUA; L. L. Patterson to A. B. Butts, April 26, 1935, annual report of the School of Engineering, MSUA; *Catalog, 1933-34,* p. 60.

3. Kenneth Withington to A. B. Butts, April 17, 1935, filed with annual and biennial reports; R. C. Carpenter to Hugh Critz, May 12, 1934, annual report of the Department of Mechanical Engineering, MSUA; L. L. Patterson to A. B. Butts, April 26, 1935, annual report of the School of Engineering, MSUA; *Catalog, 1933-34,* p. 60.

4. L. L. Patterson to D. G. Humphrey, May 13, 1936, annual report of the School of Engineering, MSUA.

5. L. L. Patterson to A. B. Butts, April 26, 1935, annual report of the School of Engineering; L. L. Patterson to G. D. Humphrey, May 11, 1939, filed with annual and biennial reports, MSUA.

6. *Catalog,* 1933-34, pp. 64-65; T. L. Hogan, "Aeronautical Department," *Alumnus* 13:2 (April 1938) 7.

7. Eric C. Clark, "Legislative Adoption of BAWI, 1936," *Journal of Mississippi History,* 52:4 (November 1990), 283-86.

8. Ernest L. Lucas to G. D. Humphrey, May 14, 1936, and L. L. Patterson to G. D. Humphrey, May 11, 1939, filed in annual and biennial reports, MSUA.

9. *Biennial Report,* 1936-37, p. 31.

10. Dewey McCain to G. D. Humphrey, May 6, 1938, and Dewey McCain to L. L. Patterson, May 5, 1938, filed in annual and biennial reports, MSUA.

11. For a lucid discussion of these issues, see W. E. Wickenden, "Preliminary Report to the Board of Investigation and Coordination and the Society," in Society for the Promotion of Engineering Education, *Report of the Investigation of Engineering Education, 1923-1929,* 2 vols. (Pittsburgh: University of Pittsburgh, 1930), 1:71-80. This massive study is commonly known as the "Wickenden Report."

12. "Wickenden Report," p. 74.

13. Paul Starr, *The Social Transformation of American Medicine* (New York: Basic Books, 1982), p. 121.

14. Starr, *American Medicine*, pp. 116-21.

15. Otis E. Lancaster, "The Future of Engineering Education in Land-Grant Universities," in G. Lester Anderson, ed., *Land-Grant Universities and Their Continuing Challenge* (East Lansing: Michigan State University Press, 1976), p. 109; M. E. McIver to Buz Walker, December 8, 1926; Buz Walker to M. E. McIver, December 17, 1926, Walker Correspondence, MSUA.

16. Charles F. Scott, chairman, Board of Investigation and Coordination, Society for the Promotion of Engineering Education, "Inception of the Project," in Society for the Promotion of Engineering Education, *Report of the Investigation of Engineering Education, 1923-1929* 1:1, 3, 6; Lancaster, "Future of Engineering Education," p. 109.

17. Twenty-Sixth Annual Report of the Engineers' Council for Professional Development, "Accredited Curricula Leading to First Degrees in Engineering in the United States, 1958," p. 28. The ECPD is now known as the Accreditation Board for Engineering Technology (ABET).

18. ECPD, "Accredited Curricula," p. 28.

19. G. D. Humphrey to Board of Trustees of Higher Learning, June 29, 1937, Humphrey Papers, Miscellaneous Materials, Box 3 (86), MSUA.

20. A. G. Holmes, "Aims and Aspirations of Mechanical Engineering for the Next Ten to Twenty Years," p. 4, A. G. Holmes Collection, Box 1, MSUA.

21. IHL, January 26, 1938, A. G. Holmes, *A Short History of the Mechanical Engineering Department of Mississippi State University of Agriculture and Applied Sciences, 1892-1976* (Mississippi State: Department of Mechanical Engineering, 1976), p. 22.

22. Robert J. Norrell, *A Promising Field: Engineering at Alabama, 1837-1987* (Tuscaloosa: University of Alabama Press, 1990), p. 107.

23. Holmes, *Short History*, p. 29; "Aims and Aspirations," pp. 11-19.

24. Holmes, *Short History*, pp. 25-26; R. C. Carpenter to A. B. Butts, April 18, 1935, annual report of the Department of Mechanical Engineering, MSUA.

25. R. C. Carpenter to L. L. Patterson, May 24, 1938, filed with annual and biennial reports, MSUA.

26. R. C. Carpenter to L. L. Patterson, May 24, 1938, filed with annual and biennial reports; G. D. Humphrey to Board of Trustees of Mississippi Institutions of Higher Learning, annual report, 1937-38, Humphrey Papers, Miscellaneous Materials, Box 4-87; L. L. Patterson to G. D. Humphrey, May 11, 1939, filed with annual and biennial reports; Martha

Strahan to R. E. Aldrich, L. M. Joyner, and H. W. Gautier, August 6, 1940, MSUA.

27. G. D. Humphrey to Board of Trustees of Institutions of Higher Learning, annual report, 1938-39, Humphrey Papers, Box 4-88, MSUA.

28. Dewey McCain to G. D. Humphrey, May 6, 1938, annual report of the Department of Civil Engineering, MSUA.

29. Robert Gay to W. H. Smith, May 15, 1918, annual report of the Department of Civil Engineering and Drawing, MSUA.

30. Dewey McCain to G. D. Humphrey, May 6, 1938, annual report of the Department of the Department of Civil Engineering, MSUA.

31. Holmes, *Short History*, p. 33.

32. A. G. Holmes to G. D. Humphrey, April 24, 1939, annual report of the Department of Mechanical Engineering, MSUA.

33. W. H. Moody to B. M. Walker, May 30, 1929, biennial report of the School of Engineering, MSUA; IHL, January 31, 1941.

34. *Catalog*, 1944-45, pp. 87-88.

35. *Annual Report*, 1945, p. 10; *Catalog, 1943-44*, pp. 17-18; L. L. Patterson to G. D. Humphrey, May 12, 1943, annual report of the School of Engineering, MSUA.

36. Although Patterson had specifically told school officials that both men and women were eligible, this was not actually the case. Mrs. Julius Ray of Pelahatchie asked President Humphrey about the program almost as soon as it was announced. "I am sure," said Humphrey, "that we will not have any courses offered for women under our present set-up." G. D. Humphrey to Mrs. Julius M. Ray, January 7, 1941, Engineering Defense Training Vertical File, MSUA.

37. L. L. Patterson to school superintendents, December 6, 1940; EDT Vertical File, MSUA.

38. Telegrams from G. D. Humphrey to J. W. Studebaker, commissioner, Office of Education, January 14, 1941; George W. Case, principal specialist, EDT program to G. D. Humphrey, January 17, 1941; G. D. Humphrey to J. W. Studebaker, January 18, 1941; R. A. Seaton, director, EDT, to G. D. Humphrey, January 21, 1941; memorandum from L. L. Patterson to G. D. Humphrey, April 28, 1941, EDT vertical file, MSUA.

39. A. A. Potter, chairman, National Advisory Committee on Engineering, Science and Management Defense Training to F. L. Bishop, secretary, S.P.E.E., University of Pittsburgh, January 9, 1942, EDT vertical file, MSUA; *Annual Report, 1945*, pp. 5-6.

40. L. L. Patterson to G. D. Humphrey, September 18, 1941; L. L.

Patterson, file memo on salaries, April 27, 1942; A. G. Holmes to G. D. Humphrey, May 20, 1942, EDT vertical file, MSUA.

41. Joseph E. Gibson et al., *Mississippi Study of Higher Education, 1945* (Jackson, Miss.: Board of Trustees, Institutions of Higher Learning, nd. [1946]), p. 389; *Starkville News*, March 31, 1944.

42. L. L. Patterson to G. D. Humphrey, April 20, 1944, annual report of the School of Engineering, MSUA; *Annual Report*, 1944, p. 3.

CHAPTER FIVE: *The Birth of a Modern College*

1. During the 1944-45 academic year a total of 2,819 students attended *all* seven of Mississippi's institutions of higher learning. Enrollments ranged from 162 at Delta State Teachers College to 872 at Mississippi State College for Women. Joseph E. Gibson et al., *Mississippi Study of Higher Education, 1945* (Jackson, Miss.: Board of Trustees, Institutions of Higher Learning, n.d. [1946], p. 389.

2. David G. Sansing, *Making Haste Slowly: The Troubled History of Higher Education in Mississippi* (Jackson: University Press of Mississippi, 1990), p. 133.

3. Gibson et al., *Mississippi Study*, pp. 40-41; L. L. Patterson to G. D. Humphrey, May 1, 1945, annual report of the School of Engineering, MSUA.

4. IHL, June 14, 1944; John K. Bettersworth, *People's University: The Centennial History of Mississippi State* (Jackson, University Press of Mississippi, 1980), p. 293.

5. *Annual Report*, 1945, p. 10; A. G. Holmes, Dewey McCain, and H. P. Neal, "Committee Report on Improving Engineering School," n.d. [April 1945], copy in annual and biennial reports, MSUA.

6. Holmes Committee Report, 1945.

7. Dewey McCain to L. L. Patterson, July 5, 1945; L. L. Patterson to G. D. Humphrey, May 1, 1945, annual report of the School of Engineering, MSUA.

8. Dewey McCain to L. L. Patterson, June 7, 1945, filed with annual and biennial reports, MSUA.

9. Gibson, *Mississippi Study*, pp. 4-6, 144-45.

10. A. G. Holmes, *A Short History of the Mechanical Engineering Department of Mississippi State University of Agriculture and Applied Sciences, 1892-1976* (Mississippi State: Department of Mechanical Engineering, 1976), pp. 54-58.

11. *Catalog*, 1946-47, pp. 94-95; *Annual Report*, 1948, p. 25.

Notes to Pages 86-93   141

12. *Annual Report*, 1948, p. 25.
13. *Catalog*, 1945-46, pp. 91-92; *Catalog* 1946-47, p. 96.
14. *Catalog*, 1945-46, pp. 92-93; *Catalog*, 1946-47, pp. 97-98.
15. *Catalog*, 1945-46, p. 94.
16. *Catalog*, 1945-46, pp. 94-95; *Catalog*, 1946-47, pp. 101-103.
17. *Catalog*, 1945-46, p. 94; *Catalog*, 1946-47, pp. 99-101; *Annual Report*, 1948, p. 25; *Starkville News*, September. 10, 1948 p. 1; *Annual Report*, 1949, pp. 21-22; interview with Harry C. Simrall by Lin Wright, December 13, 1977, MSUA.
18. *Catalog*, 1948-49, pp. 61-62; W. C. Howell to Harold Flinsch, May 16, 1949, annual report of the Department of Agricultural Engineering, MSUA; *Annual Report*, 1949, pp. 21-22.
19. *Catalog*, 1948-49, p. 118.
20. *Catalog*, 1949-50, p. 131.
21. Ibid., pp. 133-36.
22. *Annual Report*, 1945-46, p. 25.
23. James Cudworth, dean, University of Alabama College of Engineering, to O. C. Carmichael, president of the University of Alabama, November 12, 1954, in Engineering File, Carmichael Papers, University of Alabama Archives, quoted by Robert J. Norrell, *A Promising Field: Engineering at Alabama, 1837-1987* (Tuscaloosa: University of Alabama Press, 1990), p. 141.
24. L. L. Patterson, "School of Engineering," September 11, 1948, document filed with annual and biennial reports, MSUA; A. G. Holmes manuscript, p. 20, MSUA; Gibson, *Mississippi Study*, pp. 144-46; *Annual Report*, 1945, p. 10.
25. Sansing, *Making Haste Slowly*, p. 131; *Starkville News*, Sept. 2, 1949.
26. Bettersworth, *People's University*, p. 311.
27. Harold Flinsch to L. L. Patterson, June 1, 1948, annual report of the Engineering and Industrial Research Station; A. G. Holmes to L. L. Patterson, May 21, 1948, annual report of the Department of Mechanical Engineering, MSUA; *Starkville News*, September 16, 1948.
28. L. L. Patterson to Fred Tom Mitchell, June 5, 1948, annual report of the School of Engineering, MSUA; *Annual Report*, 1947-48, pp. 24-25.
29. *Annual Report*, 1948-49, p. 44; A. G. Holmes, faculty information questionnaire, January 22, 1945, MSUA.
30. Harold Flinsch to L. L. Patterson, June 1, 1948, annual report of the Engineering and Industrial Research Station, MSUA.
31. Fred Tom Mitchell to Alan T. Waterman, Chief Scientist, Office of

Naval Research, November 11, 1946, Fred Tom Mitchell Papers, United States Government (Navy) folders 1 & 3, MSUA.

32. Fred Tom Mitchell to Alan T. Waterman, chief scientist, Office of Naval Research, November 11, 1946; Fred Tom Mitchell to David Lilienthal, United States Atomic Energy Commission, May 30, 1947; Clay Lyle to Wilbur A. Lazier, director, Southern Research Institute, October 16, 1947, Fred Tom Mitchell Papers, United States Government (Navy), folders 1 & 3, MSUA.

33. Harold Flinsch to L. L. Patterson, June 1, 1948, annual report of the Engineering and Industrial Research Station, MSUA.

34. "Personal History of August Raspet," College of Engineering, Simrall Papers, box 11, MSUA.

35. Charles C. Bates and John F. Fuller, *America's Weather Warriors* (College Station: Texas A & M Press, 1986), p. 140; United States Weather Bureau, Thunderstorm Project, meetings of Thunderstorm Advisory Committee, Orlando, Florida, July 16, 17, 18, 1946, copy in Archives, Hanscom Air Force Base, Bedford, Massachusetts; Contract between Aerophysics Institute, Inc. and Office of Naval Research, June 26, 1947, copy in the office of the Department of Aerospace Engineering, MSU.

36. Holmes, *Short History*, p. 29.

37. *Starkville News*, September 16, 1949; *Commercial Appeal*, March 14, 1949; August Raspet, "Performance Measurements of a Soaring Bird," *Aeronautical Engineering Review* 9:12 (December 1950) 1-4.

38. Harold Flinsch to R. L. Hubbard, December 9, 1950, Fred Tom Mitchell Papers, United States Government (Navy) folder 1, MSUA.

39. *Annual Report*, 1949-50, p. 44.

40. A. G. Holmes to L. L. Patterson, May 7, 1949, annual report of the Department of Mechanical Engineering; Harold Flinsch to Fred Tom Mitchell, June 1, 1949, annual report of the School of Engineering, MSUA.

41. *Annual Report*, 1950, p. 41; *Annual Report*, 1951, p. 31.

42. *Catalog*, 1950-51, pp. 130-31; *Annual Report*, 1951, p. 32.

43. *Catalog*, 1950-51, pp. 132-143; *Catalog*, 1952-53, pp. 88-99.

44. IHL, October 19, 1952; *Annual Report*, 1956, p. 9; *Starkville News*, October 6, 1954.

45. *Starkville News*, April 2, 1954, June 22, 1957.

46. A. G. Holmes to Harold Flinsch, June 24, 1955, annual report of the Department of Mechanical Engineering; Harold Flinsch to Ben Hilbun, June 26, 1957, annual report of the School of Engineering and Engineering and Industrial Research and Extension Service, MSUA.

CHAPTER SIX: *The Research University*

1. Robert L. Rosholt, *An Administrative History of NASA, 1958-1963* (Washington, D.C.: U.S. Government Printing Office, 1966), p. 3.
2. Walter A. McDougall, *The Heavens and the Earth: A Political History of the Space Age* (New York: Basic Books, 1985), pp. 6-7.
3. William H. McNeill, *The Pursuit of Power: Technology, Armed Force, and Society since A.D. 1000* (Chicago: University of Chicago Press, 1982), pp. 366-69; Fredrick L. Hovde, chairman, Army Scientific Advisory Board to Wilber M. Brucker, Secretary of the Army, October 30, 1957, U.S. Senate, Committee on Armed Services, *Inquiry into Satellite and Missile Programs. Hearings Before the Preparedness Investigating Subcommittee of the Committee on Armed Services*, 85th Cong., 1st and 2nd sess. (Washington, D.C.: U.S. Government Printing Office, 1958), Senate Library volume 1270: 2293.
4. McDougall, *Heavens and the Earth*, pp. 8-9, 160-61; Maurice Pearton, *Diplomacy, War and Technology Since 1830* (Lawrence: University of Kansas Press, 1984), pp. 254-55.
5. *Inquiry into Satellite and Missile Programs*, 1958, 3:2428-30.
6. A. G. Holmes, untitled analysis of the Department of Mechanical and Industrial Engineering, 1959-60, filed with Annual and Biennial Reports, MSUA; interview with Harry C. Simrall, November 13, 1991.
7. Harry C. Simrall to Harold Flinsch, June 22, 1955, annual report of the Department of Electrical Engineering, MSUA.
8. Harry Simrall to Ben Hilbun, June 13, 1958, annual report of the School of Engineering, MSUA.
9. "Report of the Committee on Evaluation of Engineering Education," *Journal of Engineering Education* 46:1 (September 1955) 26-60; see esp. pp. 27, 35, 37, 39.
10. Interview with Harry C. Simrall by Lin Wright, December 13, 1977, MSUA.
11. Harry C. Simrall, "The Role of Colleges and Universities in Educating Future Scientists and Engineers," Conference on Utilization of Scientists and Engineers, University of Alabama, May 16, 1960; A. G. Holmes, "Aims and Aspirations," pp. 23, 28.
12. *Catalog*, 1958-59, p. 103.
13. Ibid., pp. 106-12; minutes of the Engineering Administrative Committee, August 11, 1958, MSUA.

14. Harry Simrall to Ben F. Hilbun, June 27, 1959, annual report of the School of Engineering; W. L. Everitt, president, ECPD, to Ben Hilbun, n.d. (October 6, 1959), MSUA.

15. *Inaugural Addresses of the Governors of Mississippi, 1890-1980* (Oxford: Bureau of Governmental Research, 1980), pp. 301-33; see esp. pp. 330, 332.

16. Engineering Administrative Committee, November 18, 1969, MSUA; *Jackson Daily News*, July 30, 1968.

17. *Jackson Daily News*, April 22, 1969; *Daily Herald* (Biloxi and Gulfport), April 26, 1969; *Starkville Daily News*, November 27, 1974; IHL, April 19, 1984; Willie E. McDaniel to Robert E. Wolverton, June 30, 1981, annual report of the Division of Instruction, College of Engineering, Dean's Office, College of Engineering.

18. A. G. Holmes, untitled analysis, 1959-60, MSUA.

19. Ibid.

20. A. G. Holmes, "Aims and Aspirations," pp. 20-21.

21. Harry Simrall to Ben F. Hilbun, June 27, 1959, annual report of the School of Engineering; Simrall to Hilbun, June 30, 1960, annual report of the School of Engineering, MSUA; H. S. Stillwell, chairman, Region IV, ECPD, to Harry Simrall, February 13, 1961, and Ralph Morgan, president, ECPD, to D. W. Colvard, October 3, 1962, John K. Bettersworth Papers, Engineering School, 1942-63, MSUA. Chemical Engineering probably was not accredited mainly because, until 1960, it was a branch of the Chemistry Department in the School of Arts and Sciences.

22. First Annual Report, Vice President for Academic Affairs, 1961-62, MSUA. For the procedures used by the Southern Association, see Donald C. Agnew, "Accreditation in the Southern Region," in Lloyd E. Blauch, *Accreditation in Higher Education* (Washington, D.C.: Department of Health, Education, and Welfare, 1959), pp. 64-68.

23. For an outline of Hilbun's career, see John K. Bettersworth, *People's University: The Centennial History of Mississippi State* (Jackson: University Press of Mississippi, 1980), pp. 324-38; Ben Hilbun, manuscript memoirs, MSUA.

24. "Aerophysics Department, 1949-61," p. 15, College of Engineering, Dean's Office, 1952-67, Box 1, Aerophysics Department; C. A. Moore, director, Mississippi Aeronautics Commission, to Ben Hilbun, School of Engineering, School of Engineering and Industrial Research Station, Fred Tom Mitchell Papers, Drawer 11; annual report, 1955-56, Aerophysics Department; Mississippi State Budgets, 1951-60. All are in MSUA. Interview with George Bennett, September 14, 1982.

25. Mississippi State was extremely secretive about budget matters during this period, both because the administration wished to avoid comparisons between Mississippi State and other institutions in Mississippi, and because it wished to prevent faculty members from comparing their salaries to those of their colleagues. During the 1960 self-study, for example, the administration, fearing that the misuse of budget information might produce "unfounded comparisons and general unrest," reluctantly allowed committee chairmen only to see budget information obtained directly from a dean. "Access to Budget Information in Institutional Self-Study," Bettersworth Papers, Box 38, SACS: MSU Visit, 1961, MSUA; Harold Flinsch to Herbert Drennon, February 12, 1954, Simrall Papers, Box 4, 164, MSUA. Flinsch was quoting a passage from Virgil's *Aeneid,* in which the defenders of Troy are warned against accepting the wooden horse the Greeks left as an apparent gift: "I am afraid of the Greeks even when they bear gifts."

26. "Institutional Self-Study under the Auspices of the Southern Association of Colleges and Secondary Schools, January, 1960-October, 1961," pp. v, 77, MSUA.

27. "Aerophysics Department, 1949-61," p. 7.

28. *Aviation Week,* August 5, 1957, pp. 99-104.

29. August Raspet to Bruce Carmichael, September 8, 1951, letter in the possession of Bruce Carmichael; interview with Melvin Schwartzberg, March 22, 1983.

30. "Proposal and Prospectus for an Aerophysics Institute at Mississippi State College," January 1957, pp. 9-10, Ben Hilbun Papers, Engineering and Industrial Research Station, Aerophysics Department, MSUA.

31. "Aerophysics Department, 1949-61," pp. 31-36.

32. *Mississippi State Alumnus,* June 1960, p. 24; *Starkville Daily News,* April 29, 1960; "Dr. August Raspet, A Tribute," Bettersworth Papers, Box 32, August Raspet, MSUA.

33. August Raspet to Ben Hilbun, February 19, 1957; Ben Hilbun to Jamie L. Whitten, April 5, 1957; August Raspet to Ben Hilbun, August 4, 1958, Hilbun Papers, Engineering and Industrial Research Station, Aerophysics Department, MSUA; House Concurrent Resolution number 64, 1958 legislative session; *Reflector,* November 1, 1962; interview with Harry Simrall, November 11, 1991.

34. *Aviation Week,* November 30, 1959, pp. 61-62; "Laminac Resin: A Versatile Material for Research Projects," *Plastics Newsfront* 19:2 (Summer 1963) 14-16; interview with Melvin Schwartzberg, March 29, 1983.

35. Interview with Melvin Schwartzberg, April 26, 1983.

36. McDougall, *Heavens and the Earth,* pp. 328-36.

37. Richard van Osten, "V/STOL: A Special Report," *American Aviation* (March 1965) pp. 9, 16; Research Project Reports, June 23, 1967 and July 3, 1968, in annual reports of the Engineering and Industrial Research Station, Dean's Office, College of Engineering.

38. Ben Hilbun to Joseph J. Cornish III, April 27, 1960, Hilbun Papers, Engineering and Industrial Research Station, Aerophysics Department; Franklin S. Edwards to Ben Hilbun, June 25, 1960, MSUA; *Starkville Daily News*, April 6, 1956; interview with Melvin Schwartzberg, April 26, 1983; interview with Harry Simrall, November 13, 1991; minutes of the Engineering Administrative Committee, March 13, 1967.

39. John K. Bettersworth, *People's University: The Centennial History of Mississippi State* (Jackson: University Press of Mississippi, 1980), pp. 341-42, 375-96.

40. Bettersworth, *People's University*, pp. 347-48; interview with Dean Colvard, November 14, 1991; C. V. Kirkpatrick, chairman, Region IV, ECPD to Harry Simrall, January 4, 1963, Engineering School, 1942-63, MSUA. Colvard's book, *Mixed Emotions* (Danville, Illinois: Interstate Printers and Publishers, 1985), provides a detailed discussion of the process by which Mississippi State was desegregated.

41. "Report of the Vice President for Academic Affairs," 1961-62, MSUA.

42. *Reflector*, September 26, 1961; IHL, December 18, 1980.

43. Bettersworth, *People's University*, p. 386.

44. *Reflector*, November 14, 1961; Bettersworth, *People's University*, p. 330; *Memphis Commercial Appeal* October 19, 1959.

45. Willie L. McDaniel, "A Mini Report," October 22, 1980; Harry Simrall to John K. Bettersworth, June 26, 1970, annual report of the Division of Instruction of the College of Engineering, MSUA.

46. Mississippi State University Budgets, 1959-79.

47. Mississippi State University, Fourth Annual Report of the Vice President for Academic Affairs, 1964-65; Ernst Weber, Vice President, ECPD to William L. Giles, August 1, 1968; M. R. Lohmann, President, ECPD, to William L. Giles, October 24, 1972, both in MSUA with annual reports; R. B. Beckmann, president, ECPD, to James D. McComas, President, Mississippi State, November 16, 1976, Dean's Office, College of Engineering, MSU. In 1980, the ECPD underwent internal reorganization and changed its name to the Accreditation Board for Engineering and Technology (ABET).

48. Harry Simrall to Robert E. Wolverton, June 15, 1978, annual report of the Division of Instruction, College of Engineering, Dean's Office,

College of Engineering; Mississippi State University Budgets, 1959-78; McDaniel, "College of Engineering." Willie McDaniel to Robert Wolverton, June 30, 1979, annual report of the Division of Instruction, Dean's Office, College of Engineering, MSU.

49. Charles B. Cliett to Harry Simrall, June 10, 1976, annual report for the Department of Aerophysics and Aerospace Engineering, Dean's Office, College of Engineering, MSU.

50. *Reflector,* May 3, 1961.

51. *Alumnus* (Spring 1982), pp. 13-14.

52. Willie McDaniel to Marion T. Loftin, June 19, 1980, annual report of the Engineering and Industrial Research Station; Willie McDaniel to Robert Wolverton, June 30, 1983, annual report of the Division of Instruction, College of Engineering. For a list of the type of research conducted by the DIAL program, see its annual report for the Engineering and Industrial Research Station, 1987 and 1988, Dean's Office, College of Engineering, MSU; *Starkville Daily News,* February 20, 1990.

53. Interview with Joe Thompson, November 4, 1991; John Paulk, director, Engineering and Industrial Research Station, to Willie McDaniel, June 30, 1982, annual report of the Engineering and Industrial Research Station, Dean's Office, College of Engineering, MSU.

54. IHL, December 15, 1988; interview with Joe Thompson, November 4, 1991.

55. *Flying,* June, 1981, p. 47.

56. *Starkville Daily News,* September 16, 1988, February 11, 1989, August 3, 1989; annual report of the Department of Aerospace Engineering, 1989, Dean's Office, College of Engineering, MSU.

57. Interview with Joe Thompson, November 4, 1990; annual report of the Department of Aerospace Engineering, 1989; annual report of the College of Engineering, 1990, Dean's Office, College of Engineering, MSU.

58. *Field Points,* Summer, 1991, p. 1.

Bibliography

ARCHIVAL MATERIALS

Mississippi State University Archives

MANUSCRIPTS

Minutes of the Board of Trustees of the Agricultural and Mechanical College of Mississippi, 1878-1910.
Minutes of the Board of Trustees of Mississippi State Institutions of Higher Learning, 1930-1968.
Minutes of the Engineering Administrative Committee of the College of Engineering, 1961-1969.
Annual Reports of the President of Mississippi A & M College, Mississippi State College and Mississippi State University, 1880-1965.
Annual Reports of the Vice President for Academic Affairs, Mississippi State University, 1961-1975.
Annual and Biennial Reports of the College of Engineering and its antecedents, Mississippi State University, 1891-1968.
Mississippi State University, President's Recommendations to the Board of Trustees of Higher Learning, 1930-1991.

COLLEGE OF ENGINEERING DEPARTMENTAL PAPERS

MANUSCRIPT COLLECTIONS
John Knox Bettersworth
Herbert Drennon
John Crumpton Hardy
Benjamin F. Hilbun
Alester Garden Holmes
Stephen D. Lee

Willie McDaniel
Harry Simrall
John C. Stennis
John Marshall Stone
Buz M. Walker

INSTITUTIONAL SELF-STUDIES
"The Status of the Senior-College Science-Engineering Divisions of Mississippi's Educational System—One Part of a Report on Mississippi's Space-Related Potential," Bureau of Business and Economic Research, School of Business and Industry, Mississppi State University, July, 1963.
"MSU: Its Present and Projected Role and Scope, 1965-1980."
Institutional Self-Studies Conducted for the Southern Association of Colleges and Schools and SACS Reports on Accreditation, 1960-1983.

CLIPPING AND GENERAL INFORMATION FILES (VERTICAL FILES)

PRESIDENTS
Stephen Dill Lee
John Marshall Stone
John Crumpton Hardy
George Robert Hightower
William Hall Smith
David Carlisle Hull
Buz M. Walker
Hugh Critz
George Duke Humphrey
Fred Tom Mitchell
Benjamin F. Hilbun
Dean W. Colvard
William L. Giles
James D. McComas

ANNUAL BUDGETS, MISSISSIPPI STATE UNIVERSITY, 1880-1991

PUBLICATIONS USED IN THE MISSISSIPPI STATE UNIVERSITY ARCHIVES
The Mississippi State Alumnus, 1921-1991.
Reveille, 1898-1991.
Annual Catalogs, 1884-1991.
Biennial and Annual Reports, 1884-1991.

BIBLIOGRAPHY

ARCHIVES OF THE STATE OF MISSISSIPPI, JACKSON, MISSISSIPPI
Record Group 21, State Bond Improvement Commission

OFFICE OF THE DEAN, COLLEGE OF ENGINEERING,
MISSISSIPPI STATE UNIVERSITY
Annual Reports of the School of Engineering, 1968-1991

SELECTED BOOKS AND ARTICLES

Ahlstrom Goran. *Engineers and Industrial Growth: Higher Technical Education and the Engineering Profession during the Nineteenth and Early Twentieth Centuries: France, Germany, Sweden and England.* London: Croom Helm, 1982.

Anderson, G. Lester, ed. *Land-Grant Universities and Their Continuing Challenge.* East Lansing, Michigan: Michigan State University Press, 1976.

Armytage, W. G. H. *A Social History of Engineering.* Cambridge, Massachusetts: The M. I. T. Press, 1961.

Atherton, W. A. *From Compass to Computer: A History of Electrical and Electronics Engineering.* San Francisco: San Francisco Press, 1984.

Baily, Wendell J. *The Mississippi A & M College and the War.* Brandon, MS: Mississippi A & M Bureau of War Records, n.d.[1921].

Baker, Ray Palmer. *A Chapter in American Education: Rensselaer Polytechnic Institute.* New York: Charles Scribner's Sons, 1924.

Bettersworth, John K. "'The Cow in the Front Yard': How a Land-Grant University Grew in Mississippi." *Agricultural History,* 53: 63-70, January, 1979.

Bettersworth, John K. *People's College: A History of Mississippi State.* University, Alabama: University of Alabama Press, 1953.

Bettersworth, John K. *People's University: The Centennial History of Mississippi State.* Jackson, Mississippi: University Press of Mississippi, 1980.

Bezilla, Michael. *Engineering Education at Penn State: A Century in the Land-Grant Tradition.* University Park: The Pennsylvania University Press, 1981.

Bishop, Morris. *A History of Cornell.* Ithaca: Cornell University Press, 1962.

Boelter, L. M. K. *A History of Engineering Education in the University of California.* Everett D. Howe, ed. 1970.

Brittain, M. L. *The Story of Georgia Tech.* Chapel Hill, North Carolina: University of North Carolina Press, 1948.

Brown, E. Richard. *Rockefeller Medicine Men: Medicine and Capitalism in America.* Berkeley, California: University of California Press, 1979.

Brubacher, John S. *The University—Its Identity Crisis*. New Britain, Connecticut: Central Connecticut State College, 1972.
Brubaker, John S., and Willis, Rudy. *Higher Education in Transition: An American History, 1636-1956*. New York: Harper and Brothers, 1958.
Bulletin of the Mississippi Agricultural and Mechanical College: School of Engineering. Agricultural College, Mississippi: Mississippi Agricultural and Mechanical College, 1904.
Cabaniss, Allen. *The University of Mississippi: Its First Hundred Years*. 2nd ed. Hattiesburg, Mississippi: University and College Press of Mississippi, 1971.
Calhoun. Daniel Hovey. *The American Civil Engineer: Origins and Conflict*. Cambridge, Mass.: Technology Press, 1960.
Calvert, Monte A. *The Mechanical Engineer in America, 1830-1910: Professional Cultures in Conflict*. Baltimore: Johns Hopkins University Press, 1967.
Channell, David F. *The History of Engineering Science: An Annotated Bibliography*. New York: Garland, 1989.
Cobb, James C. *Industrialization and Southern Society, 1877-1984*. Lexington: University Press of Kentucky, 1984.
Condit, Kenneth H. *A History of the Engineering School of Princeton University, 1875-1955*. Princeton: Princeton University Press, 1962.
Daniels, George H. *American Science in the Age of Jackson*. New York: Columbia University Press, 1968.
Department of the Interior, Office of Education. *Survey of Land-Grant Colleges and Universities*. Bulletin Number 9. Washington, DC: Department of the Interior, Office of Education, 1930.
Dethloff, Henry C. *A Centennial History of Texas A&M University, 1876-1976*. College Station, Texas: Texas A&M University Press, 1975.
Eddy, Edward D. *The Land-Grant Movement: A Capsule History of the Educational Revolution which Established Colleges for all the People*. Washington, D.C.: American Association of Land-Grant Universities, 1962.
Emmerson, George S. *Engineering Education: A Social History*. New York: David & Charles, 1973.
The Engineer: His Preparation and Work. Special Bulletin of the School of Engineering, 1929. State College, Mississippi: Mississippi A & M, 1929.
Engineering in Society. Washington, D.C.: National Academy Press, 1985.
First Decennial Catalog of the Agricultural and Mechanical College of Mississippi, 1880-1890. Jackson, MS: Clarion Steam Publishing Company, 1890.
Fleming, A. P. M. and Brocklehurst, H. J. *A History of Engineering*. London: A. & C. Black, 1925.

Florman, Samuel C. *The Existential Pleasures of Engineering*. New York: St. Martin's Press, 1976.
Florman, Samuel C. "The Education of an Engineer." *The American Scholar*. 55: 97-106, 1986.
Forbes, R. J. *Man the Maker: A History of Technology and Engineering*. New York: Henry Schuman, 1950.
Geiger, Roger L. *To Advance Knowledge: The Growth of American Research Universities, 1900-1940*. New York: Oxford University Press, 1986.
Gregory, Malcolm S. *History and Development of Engineering*. London: Longman, 1971.
Griffin, Marvin. *Factors Influencing Engineering Enrollment*. Washington, D.C.: American Society for Engineering Education, 1965.
Hattaway, Herman. *General Stephen D. Lee*. Jackson, Mississippi: University Press of Mississippi, 1976.
Hazen, Harold L. "Relations with Regional Accrediting Associations," *The Journal of Engineering Education*. November, 1954. 45:209-13.
Hazen, Harold L. "The ECPD Accreditation Program." *"Journal of Engineering Education*. October, 1954. 45: 101-111.
Hollister, S. C. "A Goal for American Engineering Education." *Journal of Engineering Education*, September, 1952. 43: 6-12.
Holmes, Alester Garden. *A Short History of the Mechanical Engineering Department of Mississippi State University of Agriculture and Applied Science, 1892-1976*. Mississippi State, Mississippi: Mechanical Engineering Department, Mississippi State University, n.d. [1976].
Holmes, William F. *The White Chief: James Kimble Vardaman*. Baton Rouge, Louisiana: Louisiana State University Press, 1970.
Jackson, Dugald C. *Present Status and Trends of Engineering Education in the United States*. New York: Engineers' Council for Professional Development, 1939.
Jacobs, Dillard. *10^2 Years: A Story of the First Century of Vanderbilt University School of Engineering, 1875-1975*. Nashville: Vanderbilt Engineering Alumni Association, 1975.
Kinmonth, Earl H. "Engineering Education and its Rewards in the United States and Japan." *Comparative Education Review*, 30:3, August, 1986, 396-415.
Kinnear, Duncan Lyle. *The First 100 Years: A History of Virginia Polytechnic Institute and State University*. Blacksburg: Virginia Polytechnic Institute Educational Foundation, 1972.
Layton, Edwin T., Jr. *The Revolt of the Engineers: Social Responsibility and the American Engineering Profession*. Cleveland: Press of Case Western Reserve University, 1971.

Bibliography

Lee, S. D. *The Agricultural and Mechanical College of Mississippi: Its Origin, Object, Management and Results, Discussed in a Series of Papers.* Jackson, MS: Clarion-Ledger Publishing House, 1889.

Mandel, Siegfried, and Shipley, Margaret. *Proud Past—Bright Future: A History of the College of Engineering at the University of Colorado, 1893-1966.* Boulder: University of Colorado College of Engineering, [1966].

McDougall, Walter A. *The Heavens and the Earth: A Political History of the Space Age.* New York: Basic Books, 1985.

McGivern, James Gregory. *The First Hundred Years of Engineering Education in the United State (1807-1907).* Spokane: Gonzaga University Press, 1960.

McLemore, Richard Aubrey. *A History of Mississippi.* 2 vol. Jackson, Mississippi: University and College Press of Mississippi, 1973.

McMahon, A. Michael. *The Making of a Profession: A Century of Electrical Engineering in America.* New York: Institute of Electrical and Electronics Engineers Press, 1984.

McMath, Robert C. et al. *Engineering the New South: Georgia Tech, 1885-1985.* Athens, Georgia: University of Georgia Press, 1985.

Merritt, Raymond H. *Engineering in American Society, 1850-1875.* Lexington, Kentucky: University of Kentucky Press, 1969.

Mills, Gary B. *Of Men and Rivers: The Story of the Vicksburg District.* Vicksburg, Mississippi: Corps of Engineers, 1978.

Morgan, Robert P. *Science and Technology for Development: The Role of U.S. Universities.* New York: Pergamon Press, 1979.

National Association of State Universities and Land-Grant Colleges. *Serving the World: The People and Ideas of America's State and Land-Grant Universities.* Washington, DC: National Association of State Universities and Land-Grant Colleges, [1987].

"Report of the Committee on Evaluation of Engineering Education." *The Journal of Engineering Education*, September, 1955. 46: 26-59.

Rezneck, Samuel. *Education for a Technological Society: A Sesquicentennial History of Rensselaer Polytechnic Institute.* Troy, New York: Rensselaer Polytechnic Institute, 1968.

Rosenberg, Nathan. *Perspectives on Technology.* Cambridge: Cambridge University Press, 1976.

Rudolph, Frederick. *The American College and University: A History.* New York: Alfred A. Knopf, 1962.

Sanger, George P. *Statutes at Large, Treaties, and Proclamations of the United States of American from December 5, 1859 to March 3, 1863.* Vol. XII. Boston: Little, Brown and Company, 1863.

Sansing, David G. *Making Haste Slowly: The Troubled History of Higher Education in Mississippi*. Jackson, Mississippi: University Press of Mississippi, 1990.

Saville, Thorndike. "Achievements in Engineering Education," *Journal of Engineering Education*. December, 1952. 43:222-35.

Society for the Promotion of Engineering Education. *Report of the Investigation of Engineering Education, 1923-1929*. Pittsburgh: Society for the Promotion of Engineering Education, 1930.

Starr, Paul. *The Social Transformation of American Medicine*. New York: Basic Books, Inc., Publishers, 1982.

Statutes at Large of the United States of America from December, 1889, to March, 1891. Washington, DC: Government Printing Office, 1891.

Walker, Eric A. and Nead, Benjamin. "The Goals Study." *Journal of Engineering Education*, September, 1966. 57: 13-19.

Wallace, Robert B., Jr. *Dress Her in White and Gold: A Biography of Georgia Tech and of the Men Who Led Her*. Atlanta, Georgia: Georgia Tech Foundation, 1969.

INTERVIEWS

Baxton, Al, April 16-17, 1992.
Bennett, George, September 14, 1982.
Carley, C. T., December 6, 1990.
Carmichael, Bruce, April 19, 1991.
Colvard, Dean, November 14, 1991.
Cornell, David, November, 1991, Various dates.
Raspet, Mildred, April 16-17, 1992.
Rogers, Jerry, December 6, 1990.
Scholtes, Robert, December 13, 1990.
Schwartzberg, Melvin, March 22, 29, April 6, 1983.
Simrall, Harry, November 11, 13, 1991.
Sparrow, Charles, November 21, 1990.
Thompson, Joe, November 4, 1991.
Walker, Nancy, March 5, 1991.

NEWSPAPERS

The Comet. Jackson, MS. 1879-1882.
East Mississippi Times. Starkville, MS. 1885-1925.
Jackson Clarion-Ledger. Jackson, MS. 1888-1990.
Reflector. Mississippi State University. 1890-1990.
Starkville Daily News. Starkville, MS. 1960-1990.
Starkville News. Starkville, MS. 1902-1960.

Index

A & M, 5–15, 18–19, 21–25, 30, 32–34, 39–46, 48, 51–58, 60, 72, 91
Accreditation, 42, 53–54, 57, 69–73, 82, 91, 98, 103, 105–06, 108–10, 118–19, 121
Aeronautical Engineering, 62–66, 76, 81, 86, 98, 106, 117–18, 125
Aerophysics Department, 95–96, 98, 102, 111–18, 122–23, 125
Aerophysics Institute, 95, 112, 115–16
Aerospace Engineering, 118, 122, 124
African-Americans, 13, 39, 119
Agricultural education, 5, 7, 9–10, 12
Agricultural Engineering, 29, 44–46, 51, 88, 98, 106, 120
Agriculture, 4–9, 11–13, 19, 21, 24, 29–30, 39, 44–46, 49–52, 60, 65, 83, 88–89, 98, 111–12
Alabama, 64, 105, 122
Alcorn University, 4, 6
American Medical Association (AMA), 56, 68, 70–71
Appropriations, 9, 11, 13, 25–26, 58, 72, 112, 116
Architectural Engineering, 46, 50–51, 84
Ard, Charles Edgar, 23–25, 27–29, 31–35, 37–41, 48–49
Army Air Force College Training Program, 76

Bailey, J. A., 7–8
Balance Agriculture With Industry (BAWI), 65

Barnes, Albert, 25–29, 34, 41, 48–49, 72
Barnett, Ross, 107, 118
Barrow, J. M., 9
Bennett, George, 122, 125
Bettersworth, John Knox, 110, 115
Board of trustees, 6–7, 11, 13, 19, 24, 33–34, 54–57, 59–62, 73, 75, 79–81, 91, 107–08, 111–12
Boatwright, Donald, 115
Boundary layer, 112–16
Brown, W. B., 36
Bryant, Glenn, 115, 117–18
Buchanan, James, 4
Burkitt, Frank, 10–12, 18
Butts, A. B., 61

Calculus, 17, 86
Camp, Sumpter, 64, 76, 78
Carley, C. T., 109, 119
Carmichael, Bruce, 114
Carnegie Foundation, 42, 69
Carpenter, Randle Churchill, 18, 35, 39, 47, 62–63, 72–73
Ceramic Engineering, 81, 119
Computational Fluid Dynamics (CFD), 122–24
Chemical Engineering, 81, 91–92, 109, 119, 121
Chemistry, 7, 20, 77, 86, 93–94, 104, 119
Civil Engineering, 5, 9, 13, 17, 25, 29–30, 33, 36, 40, 44–45, 49–52,

156

Index

58–60, 67, 78, 82, 86, 89, 91, 98, 106
Civil War, 4, 6, 24, 48
Classical education, 6–8
Cliett, Charles, 115
Cold War, 90, 100, 102–03, 120
Colvard, Dean, 118–19
Composite materials, 117, 125–26
Congress, U.S., 4, 13–14, 45, 76, 125–26
Conner, Martin S., 57
Cooley, Earl E., 72–73
Cooper, F. T., 5
Cornish, Joseph, 115–18, 123
Cotton, 6, 7, 19, 23, 28, 31, 41, 44, 48–49, 65
Critz, Hugh, 55, 58–63, 65
Cross, E. J., 122

Defense Advanced Research Projects Administration (DARPA), 124
Delta, 33
Department of Defense, 117
Depression, 49–50, 58–59, 63–64, 75–76
Desegregation, 118
Diagnostic Instrumentation and Analysis Laboratory (DIAL), 123, 125
Dormitories, 20, 39, 47
Drawing, 11, 14–18, 20, 25–26, 28, 33, 36, 44–45, 49–52, 58, 78, 81, 105
Drennon, Herbert, 112

Engineers' Council for Professional Development (ECPD), 69–73, 81, 98, 103–04, 106, 108–10, 119, 121
Edwards, T. S., 78
Eisenhower, Dwight D., 101–02
Electrical Engineering, 18, 20–21, 25, 27, 29, 31–32, 34–40, 48–49, 53, 58, 60, 78, 88–89, 91, 93, 98, 103, 106, 109, 122
Engineering Building, 25, 40, 48, 49, 52, 91, 92, 122

Engineering curriculum, 4, 7–12, 14, 17, 19, 20, 23, 27–30, 42, 46, 50–51, 62–63, 65, 67–68, 84–89, 97–99, 104–08, 110
Engineering Defense Training (EDT), 75–76
Engineering Experiment Station, 75, 82, 83
Engineering Technology, 107
Engineering, Science, and Management Defense Training (ESMDT), 75–77
Engineering, Science, and Management War Training (ESWDT), 75, 77
English courses, 7, 13, 15, 67, 76, 86, 89, 106
Enrollment, 11, 64, 66–67, 76, 78, 91–92, 97–99, 104, 119–21
Equipment, 4, 9, 10, 12, 14–16, 19, 20, 26–27, 29–30, 32, 35–36, 38–39, 41–42, 44, 46–48, 50, 52–53, 58, 63, 66–67, 71–72, 74, 79, 82–84, 87, 90, 92–93, 96, 103, 120, 125
Ethridge Chemical Engineering Building, 91, 121
Ethridge, M. P., 94
Extension Service, 32, 47, 49

Farmer's Alliance, 11
Flexner Report, 68–69
Flinsch, Harold von Neufville, 91–92, 94–97, 99, 103–05, 112, 121
Foundry, 14, 16, 18–19, 25, 29, 49, 63, 76, 87–88
Freeman, Mathew, 50–51, 58

Gay, Robert, 40–42, 74
Geology, 26, 44, 49
Georgia Tech, 63, 70
Germany, 16, 94, 100–01
Gibson Report, 79–81, 83–84, 90
Giles, William L., 118
Gladney, Thomas G., 44, 51–52, 56
Graduate studies, 15, 51, 61, 64, 72–73, 75, 90, 104, 108, 110, 114–15, 118

Grange, 11
Great Britain, 100-01
Grinter Report, 104
Gross, E. R., 46, 51
Gulf Coast, 33, 107, 108
Gwinner, Harry, 14, 16-18

Hancock, Charles, 33
Hardy, John Crumpton, 5, 22-26, 30, 32-38, 41, 54, 72
Harvard University, 8
Hightower, George R., 41-43, 54-55
Hilbun, Benjamin H., 109-12, 115-16, 118
Hilgard, Eugene, 5
Hoke, G. Robert, 119
Holmes, Alester G., 71, 73-74, 78, 81-84, 92, 95, 103, 105, 108-09, 112, 119
Honda Corporation, 125-26
Horticulture, 6, 7, 14
Hull, D. C., 18, 53, 55
Humanities, education in, 85-86, 88, 90, 97-98, 104-06
Hume, Alfred, 60-61
Humphrey, George Duke, 65-66, 71, 73-75, 77-78, 80-82, 84, 91
Hydraulics, 15, 30, 67

Inbreeding, faculty, 72-73
Industrial classes (Morrill Act), 3-5, 7, 41, 61, 80-81
Industrial Engineering, 65, 87, 119
Industrialization, 28, 30-31, 50, 65
Institute for Technological Development (ITD), 125
Ivy, H. M, 80

Japan, 100, 125
Johns Hopkins University, 68-69
Johnson, Lee H., 80
Johnson, Lyndon B., 102, 107

Kennedy, John F., 101-02

Laboratories, 19, 22, 26, 38, 48-49, 52, 63-64, 68, 71, 83, 91-92, 94, 116, 119, 121-22, 125
Land-grant colleges, 3-4, 6-7, 11, 13, 61, 77, 80, 83, 90
Lauchner, Julien H., 119
Lear, Bill, 111
Lee, Blewitt, 8
Lee, Stephen Dill, 5-8, 10-19, 21-22, 37, 39, 55, 80, 92
Lee Hall, 37, 39, 92
Legislature (Mississippi), 4, 6-7, 9-14, 19, 25-26, 42, 48, 50, 55, 58-59, 65, 72, 91, 108, 110, 112, 116
Liberal education, 4, 7-9, 60, 67, 84, 85, 97, 101, 104, 106
Library, 10, 48-49, 70, 91, 121
Lincoln, Abraham, 4
Lindbergh, Charles, 64
Longino, Andrew H., 24, 30-31
Louisiana, 53, 79, 122
Lucas, Ernest L., 65, 72
Lyle, Clay, 94

Magnetohydrodynamics, 122, 123
Manhattan Project, 101-02
Mississippi Aerophysics Vehicle with Extended Latitude (MARVEL), 116-18, 125
Massey, Walter E., 126
Mastin, Wayne, 124
Mathematics education, 4, 8-9, 12, 16, 23-24, 27-28, 46, 52-53, 67, 76, 84-86, 89, 99, 104-06, 108
McCain, Dewey, 49, 59, 67, 74, 81-82, 92-93
McDaniel, Willie L., 121, 126
McNamara, Robert, 117
Mechanic arts, 4-7, 9, 11-21, 23, 25-28, 36, 98
Mechanical Engineering, 13, 15, 19-20, 25, 28-29, 34-37, 49, 60-65, 72-73, 76, 78, 81, 87, 89, 98, 106, 108, 112, 119, 126

Index

Meridian, 6
Meyer, Lowell L., 115
Mining Engineering, 26
Montgomery, W. B., 6
Moody, Howard L., 51–52, 55–57, 75, 91
Moore, C. A., 111
Moore, J. S., 63–64
Morrill, Justin Smith, 3, 4, 7
Morrill Act, 3, 4, 7, 9, 11, 13
Murphree, David L., 115, 122–25

National Aeronautics and Space Administration (NASA), 119
National Science Foundation (NSF), 122, 126
Noel, Edmund F., 34

O'Shea, Michael V., 55–56, 80
Office of Naval Research (ONR), 93–95, 99, 112–13

Patterson, Lucious L., 38, 40, 48, 52, 57–59, 62–64, 70, 73, 76–78, 80–81, 83, 86, 91–92, 121
Patterson Engineering Laboratories, 91, 121
Peabody Report, 59–60
Petroleum Engineering, 82, 119
Physics, 7, 20, 25–26, 34, 40, 44, 48–49, 52, 76–77, 86, 91, 94–95, 98, 104, 123
Power plant, 29, 35–37, 45, 47–48, 58, 86
Preparatory department, 7–8, 32, 39

Raspet, August, 94–96, 98–99, 111–18, 122, 125–26
Reid, Clarence E., 35–40
Research, 68–71, 73–75, 82–83, 90–96, 98–99, 100–04, 106, 108–26
Roberts, Sean, 117, 118
Roudebush, G. S., 7–8
Rural Engineering, 26, 29, 45
Russell, Lee, 55

Sailplane research, 94–96, 114, 125
Salaries, 11, 14, 31–32, 39–40, 43, 51, 58–59, 71, 74, 77–78, 90–91, 93, 97, 102–04, 106–09, 120–22
School of Agriculture, 24, 44–46, 51–52, 83, 88–89, 111–12
Schwartzberg, Melvin, 118
Shopwork, 11, 14–20, 25–29, 35, 44, 48, 60, 67, 73, 83, 86–87, 105
Short-Take-Off-And-Landing (STOL), 96, 113–14, 116–17
Simrall, Harry C., 88, 103–05, 109, 116, 118, 121–22
Smith, William Hall, 41–43, 47, 53, 55
Southern Association of Colleges and Schools, 54, 56, 57, 112, 119
Soviet Union, 100, 102
Sputnik, 100–02, 104, 107
Starkville, 6, 8, 33, 47, 64, 74, 96, 110, 115–16, 118
Stennis, John C., 124
Stone, John M., 22, 25
Student Army Training Corps (SATC), 44
Sullivan, W. J. T., 7–9
Surveying, 9, 12, 15–16, 30, 44, 86–87, 89, 105

Tau Beta Pi, 54
Teaching loads, 40, 51, 59, 71, 82, 92, 97–98, 103, 106, 109–10, 121
Tennessee Valley Authority, 82
Textile School, 20, 24–25, 27, 30–31
Thompson, Joe F., 122, 124, 126
Thunderstorm Project, 95
Trotter, Donald, 124

University of Mississippi, 4–6, 10, 34, 54–56, 59–61, 78, 80, 83, 110, 112, 118, 122

Vardaman, James Kimble, 31, 54–55
Varnado, Osmond D. M., 72, 78
Vicksburg, 90

Waddel, John, 4
Walker, Buz, 12, 14, 16, 20–24, 26, 28, 34, 40, 43, 45, 49–56, 69, 71, 74–75, 115–16, 121
Walker Engineering Laboratories, 116
War Department, 44, 53–54, 63, 75
Warsi, U. A., 124
Weichardt, A. J., 18–21, 25
Wells, Graham W., 115
Whitfield, David, 124
Whitfield, Henry, 55
Wickenden, William E., 68–70, 85
Withington, Kenneth, 64, 78
Woodworking, 14, 16, 19, 26, 28–29, 67, 73
World War I, 35, 42–44, 47–49, 75, 78, 110
World War II, 49, 75, 78–79, 84–85, 88, 90–93, 96, 99–104, 120

www.ingramcontent.com/pod-product-compliance
Lightning Source LLC
Chambersburg PA
CBHW022103160426
43198CB00008B/328